KNOWING GOD

BIBLE STUDY

BOOK I

"I will put my laws in their minds and write them on their hearts."

"They will all know me, from the least of them to the greatest."

Hebrews 8:10-11

JAMES L. MILLARD

Knowing God Bible Study

Many years ago a man wanted to travel to the United States from Europe. He worked hard and saved enough money to buy a ticket on a cruise ship. It took about three weeks for the ship to cross the Atlantic Ocean. The man brought a suitcase filled with cheese, crackers and other food because he could not afford to pay for special meals. The other passengers ate all their meals in the restaurants while this man sat alone eating cheese and crackers.

He smelled the delicious food every day and longed to eat with the others, but did not have the money to pay for expensive meals. Near the end of the trip another passenger asked him, *"Why don't you come to the banquet hall and eat with the rest of us?"* The man replied, *"I had only enough money to buy my ticket, but cannot afford fancy meals."* The other passenger said, *"Didn't you know that the meals are included in the price of the ticket?"*

Many Christians feel like this man on the cruise ship. They would like to feast on the Word of God, but don't understand the amazing grace and bountiful blessings that are available to them in the Scriptures. They are trying to survive on cheese and crackers. Most Christians struggle to read the Bible. They do not know what chapters to read every day or how to meditate on the verses they read.

Learning to feed on the Word of God every day is one of the most basic and important skills new disciples need in order to grow in their love relationship with God. If you do not eat regularly it is very difficult to grow.

Knowing God Bible Study provides an easy plan and pathway for growth. It includes a daily reading schedule and short passages to focus and meditate on from each chapter. Knowing God Bible Study gives you a simple schedule and practical format that anyone can follow.

My desire is to help ordinary people learn to meditate on the Word and grow strong in their love relationship with God. I hope that this study will help you learn to feed yourself daily by spending time with God in His Word. This is foundational to becoming mature disciples of Jesus. I pray that Knowing God Bible Study will inspire your faith and help you to grow as a disciple of Jesus Christ.

CONTENTS

ACKNOWLEDGMENTS

Special thanks to my wife Masako who always edits and improves all of my writing. Also my son Noah Millard gave much good advice and was instrumental in formatting the document. And many thanks to my mother, Ruth M. Millard for her careful and tenacious editing, which is an amazing feat for a 90-year-old great grandmother!

Knowing God Bible Study

pray
Trust & Obey
Listen
Write
Read

Learning to Eat

Mothers and fathers use their hands to feed their babies. When a child is able to eat by himself or herself the parents no longer feed the child only milk. They pick up a small bite of food with their hand and put it on a plate. The child takes the food in his or her hand and puts it into his or her mouth. This is how parents teach young children to feed themselves.

They don't say, *"Now you are two years old so you take care of your own food from now on."* How could a two-year-old child know what to eat, where to get the food, or how to cook it? In the same way, I think new believers are overwhelmed when they are told, *"Now that you are a believer you must read your Bible every day."* They don't know where to begin.

Like children learning to eat, we must help new believers learn to feed on the Word of God. We should not just tell them to read the Bible because it is an obligation. It is important to help growing spiritual children to use their own hands to eat by themselves. We must put bite-sized pieces of Scripture on the table for them so that they can learn to have a dynamic and fruitful time in God's Word every day.

In China grandmothers wean children by chewing food for the baby and then put it into the baby's mouth. Yuk! I cannot do that for you, but I want to put some good food on the table that you can chew on and eat by yourself.

The problem is that many people don't know where to read and how to meditate on God's Word. They need a simple and doable plan. This is what we will provide for you in this study.

Learning to Meditate

This plan will help people learn to feed on the Scriptures by reading the entire New Testament and by meditating on key passages in each chapter over the course of one year. You will not completely understand some verses that you read, but it is good to read them and to begin thinking about them. However, most of the passages you will study in Knowing God Bible Study are easy to understand.

The Hand Illustration represents meditating on the Bible. You need to use all of your fingers to pick up objects, especially things that are heavy. Try picking up a pencil with one finger, two fingers, three fingers or four fingers. Of course it is much easier to use five fingers to pick up something.

The Hand Illustration shows the importance of meditating on the Word of God in various ways in order to grasp the meaning of a passage of Scripture. The five fingers in the Hand Illustration represent reading, writing, listening, trusting & obeying and praying.

The little finger represents **reading** the Bible. Reading is important, but just as it is hard to pick up something using only your little finger, if you only read a passage your understanding will be limited.

The ring finger represents **writing** down your thoughts and insights. Even if you write just a couple of sentences, writing down your ideas helps you to clarify your thoughts. This is a part of meditation.

The middle finger represents **listening** to God speak through the verses you are studying. God does speak clearly to His people through the Bible daily. It is exciting and inspiring when God speaks to you personally through the passage you are reading.

The index finger is a finger we use all of the time. We use it to write, to use telephones, to operate computers, to zip zippers and to button buttons. We would have a hard time accomplishing many things without our index finger. In the Hand Illustration the index finger represents **faith and obedience**. James 1:22 teaches, *"Do not merely listen to the word, and so deceive yourselves. Do what it says."* Unless we put into practice what we read, it is merely head knowledge. We can only obey God as we trust Him to help us.

Finally the thumb represents **prayer**. After you have meditated on the passage as described above, a very nice way to respond to God from your heart is to write a short prayer. A prayer of 2 or 3 sentences is fine. If you use all five fingers when you meditate on a passage of Scripture you will have a strong grasp of its meaning and will learn to eat spiritual food by yourself.

The purpose of your time in the Word is not just to gain knowledge or to fulfill your obligation to read the Bible. It is to love God and grow deeper in your love relationship with Him. This is the purpose of Knowing God Bible Study.

There are five parts of your daily time in God's Word as seen in the Hand Illustration:

1. **Read**
2. **Write**
3. **Listen**
4. **Trust & Obey**
5. **Pray**

Key Verse. There is a very important final step that will also be a huge blessing to you! At the bottom of each page is a key verse from the chapter you read. Write this verse down and carry it throughout the day to help you memorize it and meditate on it.

"I will put my laws in their minds and write them on their hearts."

"They will all know me, from the least of them to the greatest."

Hebrews 8:10, 11

How will Knowing God Bible Study be a Blessing to You?

If you are faithful to spend time with God every day you will receive many blessings which include the following:

Meet God every day in the Word.

Grow in your love relationship with God.

Understand the basic teachings of the New Testament.

Develop the ability to meditate on any passage in the Bible.

Learn how to hear God speak through the Bible.

Grow strong as a disciple of Jesus.

 # Simple Plan

The plan is simple and doable. You will read 1 chapter and focus on a short passage each day. You will read the entire New Testament in one year by reading 5 chapters each week. Every day you will meditate on a few verses from each chapter you read. Over the course of the year you will gain a basic understanding of many important teachings in the New Testament.

Who is Knowing God Bible Study for?

Knowing God Bible Study is a simple approach to Bible study for anyone who is hungry to grow in Christ including:

New Believers

Mothers & Fathers

Students

Young People

Busy People

People who want to learn to meditate on God's Word

Goal

The goal is to help ordinary people learn to meditate, understand and obey the Word of God and to grow in their love relationship with Him.

Commitment

This will take about 15 minutes a day, five days a week. If you miss a day during the week you can make it up on the weekend.

Man does not live by bread alone, but by every word

that comes from the mouth of God. Matthew 4:4

Instructions

READ. From Monday through Friday read one chapter a day following the schedule on **page 6**. As explained above, you will cover 5 chapters each week and you will complete reading the whole New Testament in one year. (If you get behind during the week you can catch up on Saturday and Sunday!)

FOCUS. A short passage from each chapter you read is provided for you to meditate on more deeply. Follow the 5 steps in the Hand Illustration and write your thoughts for each step. These five steps are explained below.

Five Fingers, Five Steps

1. **Read**. Read the passage listed 2 or 3 times to help you begin to focus on its meaning. Pray and ask God to help you understand and to speak to your heart.

2. **Write.** Think about the verses you are reading and write down your thoughts. Please answer the meditation question given for that passage. You may also write down any of your insights and observations. You may also answer the following questions: What is the main point? What is important? What did you learn? What does the passage teach about Jesus? You do not need to write a lot, but it will clarify your thinking if you write down your thoughts.

3. **Listen.** What is God saying to you through these verses? Take a few moments to listen. The Holy Spirit will speak through your heart and mind. Write down one or two sentences stating what you sense He is saying to you through the verses you are focusing on.

4. **Trust and Obey.** How will you trust and obey Jesus today? Try to write down specifically and practically how you will trust and obey the Lord from the passage you studied.

5. **Pray.** Write a short prayer. Writing a prayer is a great way to respond to the Lord from your heart as you reflect on what He has spoken to you.

Memorize one verse or more each week. One key verse for each chapter is listed at the bottom of each page. Underline these key verses in your Bible. Then the next time you read that chapter you will quickly remember that verse and what the chapter is about. Choose at least one verse to memorize each week and write it on a card so that you can review it.

Do Knowing God Bible Study TOGETHER! Everyone needs encouragement and accountability. It is very encouraging to share what you have learned and how God has spoken to you (either one to one or with others in a small group). Share with your discipleship partner or small group weekly or by texting every day!

Example of Knowing God Bible Study

Below is my study of John 7:37-39 as an EXAMPLE of how to do Knowing God Bible Study.

 # Week 2, Day 2

Read John Chapter 7. Focus on John 7:37-39.

Read: After reading John chapter 7 slowly read verses 7:37-39 two or three times. Pray and ask God to help you understand and to speak to your heart.

Now on the last and greatest day of the feast, Jesus stood and cried out, "If anyone is thirsty, let him come to me and drink! He who believes in me, as the Scripture has said, from within him will flow rivers of living water." But he said this about the Spirit, which those believing in him were to receive. For the Holy Spirit was not yet given, because Jesus wasn't yet glorified. John 7:37-39 NIV

Write: Write down your thoughts, insights and observations below.

Meditation Question: "How do we come to Jesus and drink living water?"

We come to Jesus by believing in Him and by receiving life from His Spirit who lives in us. We must be thirsty and go to Him as the only One who can satisfy my soul. He promised that the Holy Spirit would live in us and flow living water through us! Wow! What a promise!

Listen: What is God saying to you through these verses?

I sense God is trying to say the following to me: "Come to Me and drink. Come to Me for life every day. I am the only One who can satisfy your soul. Believe in Me. Let My living water flow through your heart and soul."

Trust and Obey: How will you trust and obey Jesus today?

Thirst for Jesus and come to him today. Believe Him to flow living water through me by His Spirit.

Pray: Write a short prayer.

"Jesus, thank You for inviting us to come to You and drink. Thank You for promising to flow rivers of living water through me by Your spirit. Fill me with Your Spirit every day. Flow Your love and Your life through me to everyone around me."

Key Verse

"If anyone is thirsty, let him come to me and drink."

John 7:37

Two Important Keys for Success

There are a number of reasons why people do not read the Bible:

1. It is not a priority.

2. They have no plan.

3. The Bible is boring when they read because they do not understand it.

4. They have no discipleship partner.

5. The Bible is overwhelming and seems too difficult.

6. They don't know how to hear God speak through the Bible.

7. They don't know the blessings available when we obey the Word of God.

Knowing God Bible Study speaks to some of these issues. It does give people a simple plan, which is doable for ordinary people. It gives people bite-sized pieces that are easy to understand and to meditate on. Knowing God Bible Study provides a simple pattern to follow so that people can understand the meaning of the passage and learn to hear God speak through it.

Knowing God Bible Study will help people learn to feed on the Word of God by themselves. However, there are two important keys that you must intentionally follow through on in order for this study to be successful and fruitful in your life. First, you must make **a clear commitment** to spending time with God every day, and second, you must **do the study together** with others.

1. If you want to be successful in this study you must have A PLAN and MAKE A COMMITMENT to do it.

It is essential that you make your daily time with God a priority. What people do not do when they are busy, they usually will not do when they have free time. All people have the same amount of time each day! Each day has 24 hours. During this time we eat, sleep, work, go to school, read the newspaper, do sports, surf the internet, send e-mail, use social media, watch TV, etcetera. The biggest reason we do not spend time with God is that it is not our priority.

If you want to study God's Word daily, you must choose to make it a priority. Begin by committing to spend at least 15 minutes a day with God in His Word. It is also important to have a clear PLAN. Decide the time and place you will meet with God every day. If you do not plan to spend time in the Word every day, you probably will not do it.

Are you willing to make your daily time with God a priority? YES, I will commit myself to spending 15 minutes a day with God in His Word.

_____
(sign your name)

When and where will you spend time with God each day? Write your answer below.

_____

_____

2. If you want this study to be fruitful, **DO IT TOGETHER** with others.

Few people have the discipline to read the Bible every day just because they are told that it is important. Everyone needs encouragement and accountability to develop consistency.

If you want this study to be fruitful then it is very important to do it together with others. Study the chapter for each day during the week and then share with your reading partner each week. Share whether or not you completed the daily studies for that week. Share with each other what you learned and how God spoke to your heart. Many people share what they got from their time in the Word through LINE, WhatsApp, Instagram, or other social media.

You will be mutually encouraged and motivated as you share together each week. You will find great joy as you share from the Word of God with others and also listen to them share with you. Everyone needs this kind of fellowship. Over time your relationship with God and with your reading partner will deepen through sharing the Word with one another.

Please discuss your commitment and desire to spend time with God with the person(s) you would like to study with. **List the name of the person (or persons) who agrees to do this study with you and to share together weekly:**

_____

_____

_____

BOOK 1
Thirteen-Week Reading Plan

Week 1

Day 1	John 1
Day 2	John 2
Day 3	John 3
Day 4	John 4
Day 5	John 5

Week 2

Day 1	John 6
Day 2	John 7
Day 3	John 8
Day 4	John 9
Day 5	John 10

Week 3

Day 1	John 11
Day 2	John 12
Day 3	John 13
Day 4	John 14
Day 5	John 15

Week 4

Day 1	John 16
Day 2	John 17
Day 3	John 18
Day 4	John 19
Day 5	John 20

Week 5

Day 1	John 21
Day 2	Philippians 1
Day 3	Philippians 2
Day 4	Philippians 3
Day 5	Philippians 4

Week 6

Day 1	1 John 1
Day 2	1 John 2
Day 3	1 John 3
Day 4	1 John 4
Day 5	1 John 5

Week 7

Day 1	Romans 1
Day 2	Romans 2
Day 3	Romans 3
Day 4	Romans 4
Day 5	Romans 5

Week 8

Day 1	Romans 6
Day 2	Romans 7
Day 3	Romans 8
Day 4	Romans 9
Day 5	Romans 10

Week 9

Day 1	Romans 11
Day 2	Romans 12
Day 3	Romans 13
Day 4	Romans 14
Day 5	Romans 15

Week 10

Day 1	Romans 16
Day 2	1 Timothy 1
Day 3	1 Timothy 2
Day 4	1 Timothy 3
Day 5	1 Timothy 4

Week 11

Day 1	1 Timothy 5
Day 2	1 Timothy 6
Day 3	2 John
Day 4	3 John
Day 5	Ephesians 1

Week 12

Day 1	Ephesians 2
Day 2	Ephesians 3
Day 3	Ephesians 4
Day 4	Ephesians 5
Day 5	Ephesians 6

Week 13

Day 1	Philemon
Day 2	2 Timothy 1
Day 3	2 Timothy 2
Day 4	2 Timothy 3
Day 5	2 Timothy 4

KNOWING GOD
BIBLE STUDY

WEEK 1

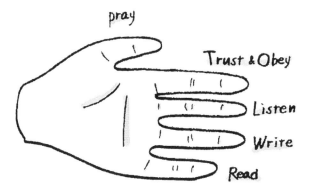

pray

Trust & Obey

Listen

Write

Read

DAY 1	JOHN 1
DAY 2	JOHN 2
DAY 3	JOHN 3
DAY 4	JOHN 4
DAY 5	JOHN 5

Introduction to The Gospel of John

Author & Date

The New Testament begins with four gospels: Matthew, Mark, Luke and John. Each gospel describes the life and teachings of Jesus. Matthew, Mark, and Luke have many similarities. The Gospel of John, however, is quite different. It records many events and teachings of Jesus that are not found in the other gospels.

Most scholars believe that John, who was one of Jesus' disciples, wrote The Gospel of John. John and his brother James were fishermen when Jesus called them to be His disciples. John was probably Jesus' closest friend. He referred to himself as, *"The disciple whom Jesus loved."* He was an eyewitness of the events that he wrote about. According to tradition, John wrote this Gospel between 60-80 A.D.

Purpose

John wrote this gospel to communicate the truth about who Jesus is. He wanted people to clearly grasp that Jesus was fully God and fully human. John wrote to make clear that Jesus is God, but He took on a human body. The eternal Word of God became a human being.

In chapter 20:31 John clearly stated his purpose for writing this Gospel:

> But these things are written that you may believe that Jesus is the Christ, the Son of God, and that believing you may have life in his name.

The word 'believe' is used 98 times in John's gospel. John wanted us to understand who Jesus is so that we will continue believing in Him. John wrote to give testimony that Jesus is the Christ, the Son of God. He repeated again and again that if you believe in Jesus you have eternal life.

Message and Main Points

Believe in Jesus

As stated above, John wrote so that people would believe in Jesus and receive life in His name. This message is found in this first chapter of John:

> Yet to all who received him, to those who believe in his name, he gave the right to become children of God—children born not of natural descent, nor of human decision or a husband's will, but born of God.   John 1:12-13

The message of John's gospel is simple and clear: Salvation is a gift of God and is received by believing. John continually emphasized the importance of believing in Jesus. John 3:16 is the most well-known verse in the Bible. It summarizes John's message of salvation through faith in Jesus:

> For God so loved the world that he gave his one and only Son, that whoever believes in him shall not perish but have eternal life.

Jesus is God

John strongly emphasized that Jesus is both God and man. This is evident from the very first verse: *In the beginning was the Word, and the Word was with God, and the Word was God* (John 1:1).

Jesus made many huge claims concerning Himself. Jesus said, *"I am the bread of life"* (John 6:35). He said, *"I am the light of the world"* (John 8:12). And, *"I am the way and the truth and the life. No one comes to the Father except through me"* (John 14:6). Jesus made several other similar statements about Himself.

Jesus plainly said that people should honor Him as they honor the Father: "That all may honor the Son just as they honor the Father. He who does not honor the Son does not honor the Father, who sent Him" (John 5: 23). The Jewish leaders wanted to stone Jesus because He claimed to be God, as recorded in John 8:58: "I tell you the truth, before Abraham was born, I am!" Eventually Jesus was crucified because of these claims.

Jesus Reveals the Father

Jesus became a human being in order to reveal to us who God is. This is clearly stated in John 1:18:

> No one has ever seen God, but God the One and Only, who is at the Father's side, has made him known. NIV

This theme is repeated again and again throughout John's gospel. For example, Jesus said, *"Anyone who has seen me has seen the Father"* (John 14:9). And, *"I and the Father are one"* (John 10:30).

John emphasized Jesus' continual focus on His relationship with His Father. The word "Father" is used in the Gospel of John more than 120 times. Jesus did everything through love relationship with His Father. John 5:19 is one example of this:

> "I tell you the truth, the Son can do nothing by himself; he can do only what he sees his Father doing, because whatever the Father does the Son also does." NIV

Jesus came to reveal the Father. He did everything through His relationship with His Father, and He came to bring us into relationship with the Father.

Jesus Commanded Us to Love and Serve One Another

Jesus was a servant. He washed the disciples' feet and told us to do likewise (John 13:1-17). He commanded us to love one another as He loved us.   Jesus said that this is the sign that we are truly His disciples.

> "Now that I, your Lord and Teacher, have washed your feet, you also should wash one another's feet. I have set you an example that you should do as I have done for you."   John 13:14-15

> "A new command I give you: Love one another. As I have loved you, so you must love one another. By this all men will know that you are my disciples, if you love one another." John 13:34-35 NIV

> "My command is this: Love each other as I have loved you." John 15:12

Outline of the Gospel of John

Hear the Word of the Lord Today!

"You search the Scriptures, because you think that in them

you have eternal life; and these are they which testify about me.

Yet you will not come to me, that you may have life."

John 5:39-40

Jesus is the center and focus of the Bible. The purpose of Bible study is not simply to gain intellectual knowledge or to understand theological principles. The purpose is to come to Jesus and to receive His life! May you come to Jesus each day in the passages you read and receive His Life!

WEEK 1, DAY 1

Read John Chapter 1. Focus on John 1:12-13.

Read John chapter 1. Then focus on verses 1:12-13. Read these verses two or three times. Ask God to help you understand and to speak to your heart.

12 Yet to all who received him, to those who believed in his name, he gave the right to become children of God – 13 children born not of natural descent, nor of human decision or a husband's will, but born of God. John 1:12-13 NIV

Write down your thoughts, insights and observations below.

Meditation Question: How does a person become a child of God?

believing on his name.

What is God saying to you through these verses?

gentiles are now included.
I am now included. so if I receive him, I'm in.
I get the forever relationship with him

How will you trust and obey Jesus today?

listening and giving a yes.
no matter what is asked of me.

Write a short prayer.

Key Verse

Yet to all who received him, to those who believed in his name,

he gave the right to become children of God.

John 1:12

WEEK 1, DAY 2

Read John Chapter 2. Focus on John 2:1-11.

Read John chapter 2. Then focus on verses 2:1-11. Read these verses two or three times. Ask God to help you understand and to speak to your heart.

¹ The third day, there was a wedding in Cana of Galilee. Jesus' mother was there. ² Jesus also was invited, with his disciples, to the wedding. ³ When the wine ran out, Jesus' mother said to him, "They have no wine." ⁴ Jesus said to her, "Woman, what does that have to do with you and me? My hour has not yet come." ⁵ His mother said to the servants, "Whatever he says to you, do it." ⁶ Now there were six water pots of stone set there after the Jews' way of purifying, containing two or three metretes (roughly 100 liters) apiece. ⁷ Jesus said to them, "Fill the water pots with water." So they filled them up to the brim. ⁸ He said to them, "Now draw some out, and take it to the ruler of the feast." So they took it. ⁹ When the ruler of the feast tasted the water now become wine, and didn't know where it came from (but the servants who had drawn the water knew), the ruler of the feast called the bridegroom ¹⁰ and said to him, "Everyone serves the good wine first, and when the guests have drunk freely, then that which is worse. You have kept the good wine until now!" ¹¹ This beginning of his signs Jesus did in Cana of Galilee, and revealed his glory; and his disciples believed in him. John 2:1-11

Write down your thoughts, insights and observations below.

Meditation Question: What did you learn from what Jesus' mother said, "Whatever he says to you, do it?"

She trusted that it was Jesus' time.

What is God saying to you through these verses?

everything Jesus touched is manifesting the best. + Mary had wild trust in him + his timing.

How will you trust and obey Jesus today?

that ultimate yes. always, always. also stepping out in small ways.

Write a short prayer.

Key Verse

"Whatever he says to you, do it."

John 2:5

WEEK 1, DAY 3

Read John Chapter 3. Focus on John 3:1-13.

Read John chapter 3. Then focus on verses 3:1-13. Read these verses two or three times. Ask God to help you understand and to speak to your heart.

¹ Now there was a man of the Pharisees named Nicodemus, a ruler of the Jews. ² The same came to him by night, and said to him, "Rabbi, we know that you are a teacher come from God, for no one can do these signs that you do, unless God is with him."
³ Jesus answered him, "Most certainly, I tell you, unless one is born anew, he can't see God's Kingdom." ⁴ Nicodemus said to him, "How can a man be born when he is old? Can he enter a second time into his mother's womb, and be born?" ⁵ Jesus answered, "Most certainly I tell you, unless one is born of water and spirit, he can't enter into God's Kingdom. ⁶ That which is born of the flesh is flesh. That which is born of the Spirit is spirit. ⁷ Don't marvel that I said to you, 'You must be born anew.' ⁸ The wind blows where it wants to, and you hear its sound, but don't know where it comes from and where it is going. So is everyone who is born of the Spirit."
⁹ Nicodemus answered him, "How can these things be?" ¹⁰ Jesus answered him, "Are you a teacher of Israel, and don't understand these things? ¹¹ Most certainly I tell you, we speak that which we know, and testify of that which we have seen, and you don't receive our witness. ¹² If I told you earthly things and you don't believe, how will you believe if I tell you heavenly things? ¹³ No one has ascended into heaven but he who descended out of heaven, the Son of Man, who is in heaven.   John 3:1-13

Write down your thoughts, insights and observations below.

Meditation Question: What does it mean to be "born again?"

saved. a new son or daughter new in a spiritual way.

What is God saying to you through these verses?

I smelt Jesus is so faithful and good. Jesus is the only way to get to the father. We also have to humble our pride.

How will you trust and obey Jesus today?

IMMEDIATE YES!

Write a short prayer.

Key Verse

"I tell you the truth, no one can see the kingdom of God unless he is born again."

John 3:3 NIV

WEEK 1, DAY 4

Read John Chapter 4. Focus on John 4:19-24.

Read John chapter 4. Then focus on verses 4:19-24. Read these verses two or three times. Ask God to help you understand and to speak to your heart.

[19] The woman said to him, "Sir, I perceive that you are a prophet. [20] Our fathers worshiped in this mountain, and you Jews say that in Jerusalem is the place where people ought to worship." [21] Jesus said to her, "Woman, believe me, the hour comes, when neither in this mountain, nor in Jerusalem, will you worship the Father. [22] You worship that which you don't know. We worship that which we know; for salvation is from the Jews. [23] But the hour comes, and now is, when the true worshipers will worship the Father in spirit and in truth, for the Father seeks such to be his worshipers. [24] God is spirit, and those who worship him must worship him in spirit and truth."   John 4:19-24

Write down your thoughts, insights and observations below.

Meditation Question: What does it mean to worship God in spirit and in truth?

ooh - good question.

What is God saying to you through these verses?

Worship is more than religion.
It should be a truthful experience of the way your spirit
feel + know to be true of the Father.

How will you trust and obey Jesus today?

Yes Yes Yes Yes.
I'll always give him my Yes.

Write a short prayer.

Key Verse

"God is spirit, and those who worship him must worship in spirit and in truth."

John 4:24

WEEK 1, DAY 5

Read John Chapter 5. Focus on John 5:39-40

Read John chapter 5. Then focus on verses 5:39-40. Read these verses two or three times. Ask God to help you understand and to speak to your heart.

39 "You search the Scriptures, because you think that in them you have eternal life; and these are they which testify about me. 40 Yet you will not come to me, that you may have life."

John 5:39-40 NIV

Write down your thoughts, insights and observations below.

Meditation Question: What is the purpose of studying the Scriptures according to these verses?

to know the Lord.

What is God saying to you through these verses?

dang. I study scriptures to know Jesus but I dont ever actually go to him? dang...

How will you trust and obey Jesus today?

Absolute, immediate yes forever and always

Write a short prayer.

Key Verse

"You search the Scriptures, because you think that in them you have eternal life; and these are they which testify about me. Yet you will not come to me, that you may have life."

John 5:39-40

KNOWING
GOD
BIBLE STUDY

Week 2

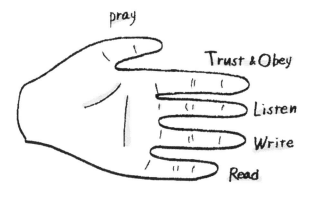

Day 1   John 6

Day 2   John 7

Day 3   John 8

Day 4   John 9

Day 5   John 10

Hear the Word of the Lord Today!

"My sheep hear my voice, and I know them, and they follow me."

John 10:27

Jesus is the Good Shepherd and He knows His sheep. They hear His voice and follow Him. Jesus is continually leading you and speaking to you! One of the main ways He speaks to you is through the Bible as you spend time with Him and read His Word daily. May you hear His words and follow Him today!

WEEK 2, DAY 1

Read John Chapter 6. Focus on John 6:26-29.

Read John chapter 6. Then focus on verses 6:26-29. Read these verses two or three times. Ask God to help you understand and to speak to your heart.

26 Jesus answered them, "Most certainly I tell you, you seek me, not because you saw signs, but because you ate of the loaves, and were filled. 27 Don't work for the food which perishes, but for the food which remains to eternal life, which the Son of Man will give to you. For God the Father has sealed him." 28 They said therefore to him, "What must we do, that we may work the works of God?" 29 Jesus answered them, "This is the work of God, that you believe in him whom he has sent."

John 6:26-29

Write down your thoughts, insights and observations below.

Meditation Question: How can we get, "Food that remains?"

advance the kingdom of God.

What is God saying to you through these verses?

grace's answer was really encouraging.

How will you trust and obey Jesus today?

Write a short prayer.

Key Verse

"This is the work of God, that you believe in him whom he has sent."

John 6:29

WEEK 2, DAY 2

Read John Chapter 7. Focus on John 7:37-39.

Read John chapter 7. Then focus on verses 7:37-39. Read these verses two or three times. Ask God to help you understand and to speak to your heart.

37 Now on the last and greatest day of the feast, Jesus stood and cried out, "If anyone is thirsty, let him come to me and drink! 38 He who believes in me, as the Scripture has said, from within him will flow rivers of living water." 39 But he said this about the Spirit, which those believing in him were to receive. For the Holy Spirit was not yet given, because Jesus wasn't yet glorified.

John 7:37-39

Write down your thoughts, insights and observations below.

Meditation Question: How can we come to Jesus and drink living water?

What is God saying to you through these verses?

full satisfaction happy

How will you trust and obey Jesus today?

Write a short prayer.

Key Verse

"If anyone is thirsty, let him come to me and drink!"

John 7:37

WEEK 2, DAY 3

Read John Chapter 8. Focus on John 8:12.

Read John chapter 8. Then focus on verses 8:12. Read this verse two or three times. Ask God to help you understand and to speak to your heart.

Again, therefore, Jesus spoke to them, saying, "I am the light of the world. He who follows me will not walk in the darkness, but will have the light of life."

John 8:12

Write down your thoughts, insights and observations below.

Meditation Question: What did Jesus mean when he said, "I am the light of the world?" What does it mean for you?

What is God saying to you through these verses?

How will you trust and obey Jesus today?

Write a short prayer.

Key Verse

"I am the light of the world. He who follows me will not

walk in the darkness, but will have the light of life."

John 8:12

Week 2, Day 4

Read John Chapter 9. Focus on John 9:1-5.

Read John chapter 9. Then focus on verses 9:1-5. Read these verses two or three times. Ask God to help you understand and to speak to your heart.

1 As he passed by, he saw a man blind from birth. 2 His disciples asked him, "Rabbi, who sinned, this man or his parents, that he was born blind?" 3 Jesus answered, "This man didn't sin, nor did his parents; but, that the works of God might be revealed in him. 4 I must work the works of him who sent me while it is day. The night is coming, when no one can work. 5 While I am in the world, I am the light of the world."

John 9:1-5

Write down your thoughts, insights and observations below.
Meditation Question: What was the assumption of the disciples about this man's sickness? How was Jesus' perspective different?

What is God saying to you through these verses?

How will you trust and obey Jesus today?

Write a short prayer.

Key Verse

"This man didn't sin, nor did his parents; but,
that the works of God might be revealed in him."

John 9:3

WEEK 2, DAY 5

Read John Chapter 10. Focus on John 10:27-30.

Read John chapter 10. Then focus on verses 10:27-30. Read these verses two or three times. Ask God to help you understand and to speak to your heart.

27 My sheep hear my voice, and I know them, and they follow me. 28 I give eternal life to them. They will never perish, and no one will snatch them out of my hand. 29 My Father who has given them to me is greater than all. No one is able to snatch them out of my Father's hand. 30 I and the Father are one."

John 10:27-30.

Write down your thoughts, insights and observations below.

Meditation Question: What do these verses teach about sheep and their Shepherd?

What is God saying to you through these verses?

How will you trust and obey Jesus today?

Write a short prayer.

Key Verse

"My sheep hear my voice, and I know them, and they follow me."

John 10:27

KNOWING GOD

BIBLE STUDY

Week 3

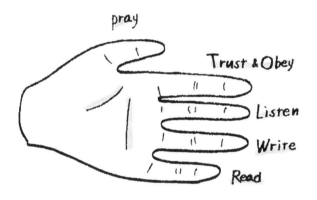

pray

Trust & Obey

Listen

Write

Read

Day 1	John 11
Day 2	John 12
Day 3	John 13
Day 4	John 14
Day 5	John 15

HEAR THE WORD OF THE LORD TODAY!

Whoever has my commands and obeys them, he is the one who loves me.

He who loves me will be loved by my Father, and I too will love him

and show myself to him.

John 14:21

If we love Jesus we will obey His commands. Then we will experience more and more of His love, and more and more of the Father's love. Also, Jesus promised that when we love Him and obey His commandments that He will reveal Himself to us! He said, *"I will show myself to him."* What an incredible promise! May God pour out His love upon you and reveal Himself to you as you love Jesus and obey His commands.

WEEK 3, DAY 1

Read John Chapter 11. Focus on John 11:25-26.

Read John chapter 11. Then focus on verses 11:25-26. Read these verses two or three times. Ask God to help you understand and to speak to your heart.

Jesus said to her, "I am the resurrection and the life. He who believes in me will still live, even if he dies. Whoever lives and believes in me will never die. Do you believe this?"

John 11:25-26

Write down your thoughts, insights and observations below.
Meditation Question: Do you believe that Jesus is the resurrection and the life and that you will never die?

What is God saying to you through these verses?

How will you trust and obey Jesus today?

Write a short prayer.

Key Verse

"I am the resurrection and the life. He who believes in me will still live, even if he dies."

John 11:25

WEEK 3, DAY 2

Read John Chapter 12. Focus on John 12:1-8.

Read John chapter 12. Then focus on verses 12:1-8. Read these verses two or three times. Ask God to help you understand and to speak to your heart.

¹ Then six days before the Passover, Jesus came to Bethany, where Lazarus was, who had been dead, whom he raised from the dead. ² So they made him a supper there. Martha served, but Lazarus was one of those who sat at the table with him. ³ Then Mary took a pound of ointment of pure nard, very precious, and anointed Jesus's feet and wiped his feet with her hair. The house was filled with the fragrance of the ointment.
⁴ Then Judas Iscariot, Simon's son, one of his disciples, who would betray him, said, ⁵ "Why wasn't this ointment sold for three hundred denarii, and given to the poor?" ⁶ Now he said this, not because he cared for the poor, but because he was a thief, and having the money box, used to steal what was put into it. ⁷ But Jesus said, "Leave her alone. She has kept this for the day of my burial. ⁸ For you always have the poor with you, but you don't always have me."
John 12:1-8

Write down your thoughts, insights and observations below.
Meditation Question: Why do you think Mary anointed Jesus with the expensive perfume?

What is God saying to you through these verses?

How will you trust and obey Jesus today?

Write a short prayer.

Key Verse

The house was filled with the fragrance of the ointment.

John 12:3

WEEK 3, DAY 3

Read John Chapter 13. Focus on John 13:34-35.

Read John chapter 13. Then focus on verses 13:34-35. Read these verses two or three times. Ask God to help you understand and to speak to your heart.

³⁴ "A new command I give you: Love one another. As I have loved you, so you must love one another. ³⁵ By this all men will know that you are my disciples, if you love one another."

John 13:34-35

Write down your thoughts, insights and observations below.
Meditation Question: Do people know that we are His disciples by our love for one another?

What is God saying to you through these verses?

How will you trust and obey Jesus today?

Write a short prayer.

Key Verse

"A new command I give you: Love one another. As I have loved you, so you must love one another. By this all men will know that you are my disciples, if you love one another."

John 13:34-35

Week 3, Day 4

Read John Chapter 14. Focus on John 14:21.

Read John chapter 14. Then focus on verses 14:21. Read these verses two or three times. Ask God to help you understand and to speak to your heart.

"Whoever has my commands and obeys them, he is the one who loves me. He who loves me will be loved by my Father, and I too will love him and show myself to him."

John 14:21 NIV

Write down your thoughts, insights and observations below.
        Meditation Question: What promises did Jesus give in these verses to those who love Jesus and obey his commands?

What is God saying to you through these verses?

How will you trust and obey Jesus today?

Write a short prayer.

Key Verse

"Whoever has my commands and obeys them, he is the one who loves me. He who loves me will be loved by my Father, and I too will love him and show myself to him."

John 14:21

WEEK 3, DAY 5

Read John Chapter 15. Focus on John 15:4-5.

Read John chapter 15. Then focus on verses 15:4-5. Read these verses two or three times. Ask God to help you understand and to speak to your heart.

4 Remain in me, and I in you. As the branch can't bear fruit by itself unless it remains in the vine, so neither can you, unless you remain in me. 5 I am the vine. You are the branches. He who remains in me and I in him bears much fruit, for apart from me you can do nothing.

John 15:4-5

Write down your thoughts, insights and observations below.

Meditation Question: What does it mean to "remain" in Jesus?

What is God saying to you through these verses?

How will you trust and obey Jesus today?

Write a short prayer.

Key Verse

"I am the vine. You are the branches. He who remains in me and I in him
bears much fruit, for apart from me you can do nothing."

John 15:5

43

KNOWING
GOD
BIBLE STUDY

WEEK 4

Day 1	John 16
Day 2	John 17
Day 3	John 18
Day 4	John 19
Day 5	John 20

Hear the Word of the Lord Today!

However when he, the Spirit of truth, has come, he will guide you
into all truth, for he will not speak from himself; but whatever he hears,
he will speak. He will declare to you things that are coming.

John 16:13

Jesus gave the Holy Spirit to live in every believer and He promised that the Spirit would guide us into all truth.   When you read the Bible the Holy Spirit is active in your heart and in your mind to help you understand. God speaks to us through the Holy Spirit as we meditate on the Scriptures. Open your heart to the Holy Spirit when you read the Bible and trust Him to speak to you.

WEEK 4, DAY 1

Read John Chapter 16. Focus on John 16:13.

Read John chapter 16. Then focus on verse 16:13. Read these verses two or three times. Ask God to help you understand and to speak to your heart.

However when he, the Spirit of truth, has come, he will guide you into all truth, for he will not speak from himself; but whatever he hears, he will speak. He will declare to you things that are coming.

John 16:13

Write down your thoughts, insights and observations below.
Meditation Question: What does this verse teach about how the Holy Spirit will work in our lives?

What is God saying to you through these verses?

How will you trust and obey Jesus today?

Write a short prayer.

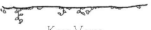

Key Verse
"However when he, the Spirit of truth, has come, he will guide you into all truth, for he will not speak from himself; but whatever he hears, he will speak. He will declare to you things that are coming."
John 16:13

Week 4, Day 2

Read John Chapter 17. Focus on John 17:20-23.

Read John chapter 17. Then focus on verses 17:20-23. Read these verses two or three times. Ask God to help you understand and to speak to your heart.

20 Not for these only do I pray, but for those also who will believe in me through their word, 21 that they may all be one; even as you, Father, are in me, and I in you, that they also may be one in us; that the world may believe that you sent me. 22 The glory which you have given me, I have given to them; that they may be one, even as we are one; 23 I in them, and you in me, that they may be perfected into one; that the world may know that you sent me and loved them, even as you loved me.

John 17:20-23

Write down your thoughts, insights and observations below.

Meditation Question: According to these verses how will we become one?

What is God saying to you through these verses?

How will you trust and obey Jesus today?

Write a short prayer.

Key Verse
"Not for these only do I pray, but for those also who will believe in me through their word, that they may all be one; even as you, Father, are in me, and I in you, that they also may be one in us; that the world may believe that you sent me."
John 17:20-21

WEEK 4, DAY 3

Read John Chapter 18. Focus on John 18:11.

Read John chapter 18. Then focus on verses 18:11. Read these verses two or three times. Ask God to help you understand and to speak to your heart.

Jesus therefore said to Peter, "Put the sword into its sheath. The cup which the Father has given me, shall I not surely drink it?"

John 18:11

Write down your thoughts, insights and observations below.
        Meditation Question: What was Jesus' attitude towards being arrested and going to the cross?

What is God saying to you through these verses?

How will you trust and obey Jesus today?

Write a short prayer.

Key Verse

Jesus therefore said to Peter, "Put the sword into its sheath. The cup which the Father has given me, shall I not surely drink it?"

John 18:11

WEEK 4, DAY 4

Read John Chapter 19. Focus on John 19:30.

Read John chapter 19. Then focus on verses 19:30. Read these verses two or three times. Ask God to help you understand and to speak to your heart.

When Jesus therefore had received the vinegar, he said, "It is finished."

He bowed his head, and gave up his spirit.

John 19:30

Write down your thoughts, insights and observations below.

Meditation Question: What did Jesus mean when He said, "It is finished?"

What is God saying to you through these verses?

How will you trust and obey Jesus today?

Write a short prayer.

Key Verse

"It is finished."

John 19:30

WEEK 4, DAY 5

Read John Chapter 20. Focus on John 20:31.

Read John chapter 20. Then focus on verses 20:31. Read these verses two or three times. Ask God to help you understand and to speak to your heart.

But these are written, that you may believe that Jesus is the Christ, the Son of God, and that believing you may have life in his name.

John 20:31

Write down your thoughts, insights and observations below.
Meditation Question: How have you come to believe more in Jesus from reading the Gospel of John?

What is God saying to you through these verses?

How will you trust and obey Jesus today?

Write a short prayer.

Key Verse

But these are written, that you may believe that Jesus is the Christ, the
Son of God, and that believing you may have life in his name.

John 20:31

KNOWING GOD

BIBLE STUDY

Week 5

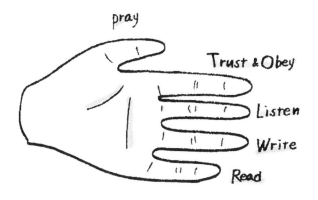

Day 1	John 21
Day 2	Philippians 1
Day 3	Philippians 2
Day 4	Philippians 3
Day 5	Philippians 4

Introduction to Philippians

Author and Date

The city of Philippi was named after King Philip II of Macedonia in 356 B.C. who was the father of Alexander the Great. It became a colony of Rome in 42 B.C. and enjoyed political and economic prosperity. It was located on the main road connecting the eastern provinces with Rome known as the Egnation Way.

The church in Philippi was established through the clear leading and work of the Holy Spirit. Paul saw a vision of a man from Macedonia begging him to come (Acts 16:6-10). Through this vision Paul and his companions (Silas, Timothy, Luke and possibly others) knew that God wanted them to preach the gospel in the region.

Paul and his companions made their way to Philippi. Acts 16:11-40 describes their ministry there. Lydia was the first one in that city to believe the gospel. Later, however, Paul and Silas were thrown into jail for casting a demon out of a girl who predicted the future through an evil spirit. In jail Paul and Silas were praying and worshiping God about midnight when God shook the jail with a great earthquake. The doors of the jail flew open and the chains fell off the prisoners.

The jailer almost killed himself because he thought that the prisoners had escaped.   When he found that they were all there, he came to Paul and Silas and asked the question, *"What must I do to be saved?"* Paul answered, *"Believe in the Lord Jesus, and you will be saved - you and your household"* (Acts 16:31). The jailer and all his family were baptized that night. These episodes show how the church in Philippi was formed through the powerful work of God in people's lives.

Most scholars believe that Paul wrote this letter to the church in Philippi while imprisoned in Rome. He probably composed the letter while under house arrest awaiting trial as described in Acts 28:14-31.   If this is the case, the date of the writing would be in 61 or 62 A.D. Paul and his missionary team had planted the church in Philippi some ten or eleven years before this time.

Purpose

The church in Philippi had kept in contact with Paul. When they learned of his imprisonment they sent a financial gift to him through one of their members whose name was Epaphroditus. After Epaphroditus delivered the gift to Paul he became very sick and almost died. Upon his recovery Paul sent him back to the church in Philippi with a letter for them.

Paul wanted to thank them for their encouragement and financial support. In addition to telling them about his own situation, he also took the occasion to encourage them in their walk with Christ.   Paul also explained to them why he was sending Epaphroditus back to them and warned them about false teachers. This letter reflects the intimate and warm personal relationship that Paul had with believers in Philippi.

Message and Main Points

Knowing Christ and experiencing His life and power is the central focus of Paul's message to the church in Philippi.   The word "Christ" is used 38 times in this short letter.   Each chapter speaks about our life in Christ and the wonderful blessings that are ours in Him.

Other significant themes in Philippians include joy, fellowship, humility and unity. Paul expressed his joy and faith in the Lord and also instructed them to, *rejoice in the Lord always.*   He demonstrated by his life and example that joy is not dependent on circumstances, but on our relationship with the Lord. He was able to rejoice despite his imprisonment and suffering.

"Fellowship" is another word that reoccurs frequently in Philippians.   A spirit of humility, which Christ modeled for us, maintains unity in fellowship. Paul also expressed his appreciation for their financial gifts in this letter. Apparently the church in Philippi was Paul's strongest supporting church.

Outline of Philippians

Philippians 1.   Christ is Our Life

"For to me, to live is Christ and to die is gain."

Philippians 2.   Christ is Our Model

"Your attitude should be the same as that of Christ Jesus."

Philippians 3.   Christ is Our Goal

"I want to know Christ and the power of his resurrection."

Philippians 4.   Christ is Our Strength

"I can do everything through him who gives me strength."

Hear the Word of the Lord Today!

But these are written that you may believe that Jesus is the Christ,

the Son of God, and that by believing you may have life in his name.

John 20:31

The purpose of John's Gospel is that we believe in Jesus and have life in His name. God wants us to not just analyze and understand the Scriptures intellectually, but to hear with our hearts and to respond to Him in faith. The entire Bible points us to Jesus. When we hear the Word of God and believe we receive the life of Jesus. May you receive His life today and every day as you hear and believe the Word of God.

WEEK 5, DAY 1

Read John Chapter 21. Focus on John 21:15-17.

Read John chapter 21. Then focus on verses 21:15-17. Read these verses two or three times. Ask God to help you understand and to speak to your heart.

15 So when they had eaten their breakfast, Jesus said to Simon Peter, "Simon, son of Jonah, do you love me more than these?" He said to him, "Yes, Lord; you know that I have affection for you." He said to him, "Feed my lambs."
16 He said to him again a second time, "Simon, son of Jonah, do you love me?" He said to him, "Yes, Lord; you know that I have affection for you." He said to him, "Tend my sheep."
17 He said to him the third time, "Simon, son of Jonah, do you have affection for me?" Peter was grieved because he asked him the third time, "Do you have affection for me?" He said to him, "Lord, you know everything. You know that I have affection for you."
Jesus said to him, "Feed my sheep.   John 21:15-17

Write down your thoughts, insights and observations below.
Meditation Question: How will you respond if Jesus asks you the same question He asked Peter, "Do you love Me?"

What is God saying to you through these verses?

How will you trust and obey Jesus today?

Write a short prayer.

Key Verse
"Simon, son of Jonah, do you love me?"
John 21:16

Week 5, Day 2

Read Philippians Chapter 1. Focus on Philippians 1:19-21.

Read Philippians 1. Then focus on verses 1:19-21. Read these verses two or three times. Ask God to help you understand and to speak to your heart.

¹⁹ For I know that this will turn out to my salvation, through your prayers and the supply of the Spirit of Jesus Christ, ²⁰ according to my earnest expectation and hope, that I will in no way be disappointed, but with all boldness, as always, now also Christ will be magnified in my body, whether by life or by death. ²¹ For to me to live is Christ, and to die is gain.

Philippians 1:19-21

Write down your thoughts, insights and observations below.

Meditation Question: What was Paul's greatest desire and main focus?

What is God saying to you through these verses?

How will you trust and obey Jesus today?

Write a short prayer.

Key Verse

For to me, to live is Christ and to die is gain.

Philippians 1:21

WEEK 5, DAY 3

Read Philippians Chapter 2. Focus on Philippians 2:5-8.

Read Philippians 2. Then focus on verses 2:5-8. Read these verses two or three times. Ask God to help you understand and to speak to your heart.

⁵ Your attitude should be the same as that of Christ Jesus. ⁶ Who, being in very nature God, did not consider equality with God something to be grasped, ⁷ but made himself nothing, taking the very nature of a servant, being made in human likeness. ⁸ And being found in appearance as a man, he humbled himself and became obedient to death—even death on a cross!

Philippians 2:5-8 NIV

Write down your thoughts, insights and observations below.
Meditation Question: What is the attitude (mind, way of thinking, values) of Jesus?

What is God saying to you through these verses?

How will you trust and obey Jesus today?

Write a short prayer.

Key Verse

Your attitude should be the same as that of Christ Jesus.

Philippians 2:5

63

WEEK 5, DAY 4

Read Philippians Chapter 3. Focus on Philippians 3:7-11.

Read Philippians 3. Then focus on verses 3:7-11. Read these verses two or three times. Ask God to help you understand and to speak to your heart.

7 However, I consider those things that were gain to me as a loss for Christ. 8 Yes most certainly, and I count all things to be a loss for the excellency of the knowledge of Christ Jesus, my Lord, for whom I suffered the loss of all things, and count them nothing but refuse, that I may gain Christ 9 and be found in him, not having a righteousness of my own, that which is of the law, but that which is through faith in Christ, the righteousness which is from God by faith, 10 that I may know him, and the power of his resurrection, and the fellowship of his sufferings, becoming conformed to his death, 11 if by any means I may attain to the resurrection from the dead.

Philippians 3:7-11

Write down your thoughts, insights and observations below.
Meditation Question: What was Paul's greatest passion and goal? What is yours?

What is God saying to you through these verses?

How will you trust and obey Jesus today?

Write a short prayer.

Key Verse

I consider those things that were gain to me as a loss for Christ.

Philippians 3:7

WEEK 5, DAY 5

Read Philippians Chapter 4. Focus on Philippians 4:6-7.

Read Philippians 4. Then focus on verses 4:6-7. Read these verses two or three times. Ask God to help you understand and to speak to your heart.

⁶ In nothing be anxious, but in everything, by prayer and petition, with thanksgiving, let your requests be made known to God. ⁷ And the peace of God, which surpasses all understanding, will guard your hearts and your thoughts in Christ Jesus.

Philippians 4:6-7

Write down your thoughts, insights and observations below.

Meditation Question: What do these verses teach about prayer?

What is God saying to you through these verses?

How will you trust and obey Jesus today?

Write a short prayer.

Key Verse

In nothing be anxious, but in everything, by prayer and petition with thanksgiving, let your requests be made known to God. And the peace of God, which surpasses all understanding, will guard your hearts and your thoughts in Christ Jesus.

Philippians 4:6-7

KNOWING
GOD
BIBLE STUDY

WEEK 6

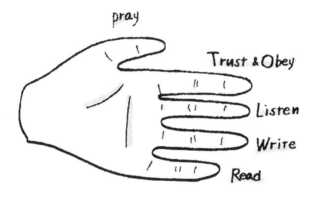

DAY 1   1 JOHN 1

DAY 2   1 JOHN 2

DAY 3   1 JOHN 3

DAY 4   1 JOHN 4

DAY 5   1 JOHN 5

Introduction to I John

In the opening words of this letter John declared that he is proclaiming to his readers something that he had personally witnessed. He had seen Jesus, the Word of life, with his own eyes and touched him with his hands. In verse 3 John states the main purpose of the letter: *"We proclaim to you what we have seen and heard, so that you also may have fellowship with us. And our fellowship is with the Father and with his Son, Jesus Christ."* John experienced real fellowship with Jesus and wrote so that his readers could experience the same intimate fellowship.

Although John does give other reasons for writing the letter, it is accurate to say that this short letter is about how to have true fellowship with God and with others. John's message can be summarized as follows: *"We will experience true fellowship with God and with each other as we walk in the light and walk in love."* He repeats this message again and again in the five short chapters.

John answers several basic questions in the letter, which most people want to find the answers to. These questions include the following:

> How can we have true fellowship with God and with each other?

> How can we know that we know God?

> Who are true children of God?

> How can we have assurance that we have eternal life?

> How can we identify true and false teachers?

The teachings in 1 John reflect the teachings found in the Gospel of John (especially in chapters 13-17). One example of this can be seen by comparing John 20:31 and I John 5:13:

> But these are written, that you may believe that Jesus is the Christ, the Son of God, and that believing you may have life in his name.   John 20:31

> I write these things to you who believe in the name of the Son of God so that you may know that you have eternal life.   I John 5:13 NIV

It is clear from these verses that the Gospel of John and the letter of 1 John are complimentary in purpose.   The gospel was written so that we might have life. The first letter of John was written so that we may know that we have life. John reveals Jesus in his gospel as the author of life. In the first letter of John he explains how we can experience that life.

Author, Date and Place

The letter of 1 John is anonymous.   The author of II and III John identifies himself as, "the elder." However, most scholars agree that all three letters were most likely written by Jesus' disciple John, who wrote the Gospel of John and referred to himself as, *"The disciple who*

Jesus loved" (John 21:20-24). In 1 John 1:1-3 the author asserts that he had seen and touched Jesus, which further supports the authorship of John. The style and emphasis of the letter also support the assertation that the author was the Apostle John.

The letter of 1 John was probably written around 80 A.D. John may have been writing to a network of house churches in or near Ephesus. John wrote about false teachings that were being spread, which will be explained below. However, his first concern was not to confront the false teachers, but to protect, guide and build up the believers he was writing to. John did make clear the errors in their false doctrines. However, he focused on teaching the believers how to discern truth from error and how to identify true followers of Christ from false ones.

John wanted to help the believers live in a genuine love relationship with God. He emphasized that this relationship is centered in the person of Jesus Christ who was truly man and truly God. Living in Him means to walk in the light and to walk in love.

Circumstances and Purpose

As mentioned above, the focus of 1 John is about living in fellowship with God and with one another. He gave three tests that reveal whether or not a person is truly living in fellowship with God. This emphasis was a response to false teachers who had been spreading error. Some of them had been a part of their fellowship, but had left (1 John 2: 18-19). They were spreading false teachings about Jesus and false teachings about the basic tenets of the Christian life.

The letter of 1 John sounds more like a series of short messages than a personal letter. However, John was trying to deal with numerous false teachings that were being spread and to make very clear to believers the essence of walking with God.

The false teachers appealed to a belief held by some people who taught that physical matter is sinful. They concluded therefore Jesus could not have had a physical body. They taught that he only had a "spirit body." Later this developed in to Gnosticism, which was a heresy that continued to challenge believers in the second and third centuries.

Some people taught that there was a distinction between the physical man Jesus and the spiritual Jesus who came upon the physical Jesus at His baptism and departed from Him before the crucifixion. Others taught that Jesus only seemed to have a physical body. 1 John was written to combat false teachings like these, which denied the incarnation and humanity of Jesus.

Most cults say that they believe in Jesus, but similarly twist and redefine the nature and work of Jesus. John emphasized repeatedly that Jesus is God who became a human being so that He could become our substitute sacrifice and die for our sins. Most cults and false teachers deny the divinity and humanity of Jesus. Often this leads them to justify sin and disobedience, which is the second test John gave to distinguish true believers from false ones. The test of love also identifies false teachers and false believers. If a person does not know God he or she cannot walk in love, because God is the source of love.

Message and Main Points

Some people say that 1 John is cyclical rather than linear in style and that its structure and message are hard to understand. However, John repeated his main points again and again so that they would be absolutely clear. Several of these central themes are listed below under the discussion of, Themes in 1 John.

There are, however, three very important points that should be absolutely clear to everyone who reads 1 John. In this letter John set forth three concrete ways to know whether a person knows God or not:

      1. Do they believe in Jesus?

      2. Do they obey God's commands?

      3. Do they love one another?

John did not give a list of theological statements for people to agree with conceptually. The tests he gave to discern whether or not a person knows God focus on the above three things. The first one emphasizes true faith in Jesus. Jesus is God and became a man in order to shed His blood for our sins. People who do not believe this do not know God. John also said repeatedly that people who do not obey His commands and who do not love others do not know Him.   John emphasizes orthopraxy as much as orthodoxy.

There are many people who say that they believe in orthodox Christian theology. However, if they do not truly believe in Jesus, do not obey His commands or do not love others, then it is clear that they do not really know God. In a world today in which people focus on particular doctrines, worship styles, church models, methods and philosophy of ministry, I think it would be wise to return to these three tests John gave: 1. Do they believe in Jesus? 2. Do they obey God's commands? 3. Do they love one another?

I John is not presented in a linear or logical order (unlike Paul's letters). Instead he repeats several core teachings many times. Repeating a key teaching again and again is a method called amplification.   John's writing style is much different from the letters of Paul. John is contemplative rather than argumentative. He is intuitive rather than logical. John emphasizes the confirmation of truth in one's life experience rather than by the intellectual acceptance of certain doctrines.

The letter of I John is characterized by its authoritative declaration of truth and denunciation of error. However, there is a continual emphasis on walking in love. John contrasts several images in order to emphasize his point. These include light and darkness, death and life, love and hate, good and evil, etc.

Themes in I John

John repeated several themes in this letter again and again. John strongly emphasized that your actions and lifestyle are what reveal the validity of your faith. Obeying His commands, especially the command to love others, is the true indicator of your relationship with God, not words alone.

Other reoccurring themes in I John include the following: Love, Fellowship, Light & Darkness, Obedience & Commands, Know, Claim/Say, Son, Spirit, Father, Death & Life, Live in/Remain in, Truth & Lies, Sin, the World, Antichrist, False Prophets, Pray/Ask, Believe, Birth & Children.

Hear the Word of the Lord Today!

If we walk in the light, as he is in the light, we have fellowship with
one another, and the blood of Jesus, his Son, purifies us from all sin.

1 John 1:7

Your word is a lamp to my feet and a light for my path.

Psalm 119:105

God guides us and speaks to us through the Scriptures. They are like a lamp shining on the path as we are walking. His word makes our way clear so that we do not stumble and so that we go the right way. May you walk in the light of His presence today! May His words be clear to you and be the light for your path.

Week 6, Day 1

Read I John Chapter 1. Focus on I John 1:5-10.

Read I John chapter 1. Then focus on verses 1:5-10. Read these verses two or three times. Ask God to help you understand and to speak to your heart.

5 This is the message we have heard from him and declare to you: God is light; in him there is no darkness at all. 6 If we claim to have fellowship with him yet walk in the darkness, we lie and do not live by the truth. 7 But if we walk in the light, as he is in the light, we have fellowship with one another, and the blood of Jesus, his Son, purifies us from all sin. 8 If we claim to be without sin, we deceive ourselves and the truth is not in us. 9 If we confess our sins, he is faithful and just and will forgive us our sins and purify us from all unrighteousness. 10 If we claim we have not sinned, we make him out to be a liar and his word has no place in our lives.

I John 1:5-10 NIV

Write down your thoughts, insights and observations below.
Meditation Question: What do these verses say about God and about fellowship with God and with each other?

What is God saying to you through these verses?

How will you trust and obey Jesus today?

Write a short prayer.

Key Verse

If we confess our sins, he is faithful and just and will forgive us our sins

and purify us from all unrighteousness.

I John 1:9

75

Week 6, Day 2

Read I John Chapter 2. Focus on I John 2:9-11.

Read I John chapter 2. Then focus on verses 2:9-11. Read these verses two or three times. Ask God to help you understand and to speak to your heart.

9 Anyone who claims to be in the light but hates his brother is still in the darkness. 10 Whoever loves his brother lives in the light, and there is nothing in him to make him stumble. 11 But whoever hates his brother is in the darkness and walks around in the darkness; he does not know where he is going, because the darkness has blinded him.

I John 2:9-11 NIV

Write down your thoughts, insights and observations below.
Meditation Question: Why do you think that if we love others we will be living in the light?

What is God saying to you through these verses?

How will you trust and obey Jesus today?

Write a short prayer.

Key Verse

Whoever loves his brother lives in the light, and there is

nothing in him to make him stumble.

I John 2:10

WEEK 6, DAY 3

Read I John Chapter 3. Focus on I John 3:16-18.

Read I John chapter 3. Then focus on verses 3:16-18. Read these verses two or three times. Ask God to help you understand and to speak to your heart.

¹⁶ This is how we know what love is: Jesus Christ laid down his life for us. And we ought to lay down our lives for our brothers. ¹⁷ If anyone has material possessions and sees his brother in need but has no pity on him, how can the love of God be in him? ¹⁸ Dear children, let us not love with words or tongue but with actions and in truth.

I John 3:16-18 NIV

Write down your thoughts, insights and observations below.

Meditation Question: According to these verses what is love?

What is God saying to you through these verses?

How will you trust and obey Jesus today?

Write a short prayer.

Key Verse

Dear children, let us not love with words or tongue but with actions and in truth.

I John 3:18

Week 6, Day 4

Read I John Chapter 4. Focus on I John 4:7-12.

Read I John chapter 4. Then focus on verses 4:7-12. **Read** these verses two or three times. Ask **God** to help you understand and to speak to your heart.

⁷Dear friends, let us love one another, for love comes from God. Everyone who loves has been born of God and knows God. ⁸Whoever does not love does not know God, because God is love. ⁹This is how God showed his love among us: He sent his one and only Son into the world that we might live through him. ¹⁰This is love: not that we loved God, but that he loved us and sent his Son as an atoning sacrifice for our sins. ¹¹Dear friends, since God so loved us, we also ought to love one another. ¹²No one has ever seen God; but if we love one another, God lives in us and his love is made complete in us.

I John 4:7-12 NIV

Write down your thoughts, insights and observations below.
Meditation Question: Why is loving others so important? Why are we able to love others?

What is **God** saying to you through these verses?

How will you trust and obey **Jesus** today?

Write a short prayer.

Key Verse

Whoever does not love does not know God, because God is love.

I John 4:8

Week 6, Day 5

Read I John Chapter 5. Focus on I John 5:11-13.

Read I John chapter 5. Then focus on verses 5:11-13. Read these verses two or three times. Ask God to help you understand and to speak to your heart.

[11] And this is the testimony: God has given us eternal life, and this life is in his Son. [12] He who has the Son has life; he who does not have the Son of God does not have life. [13] I write these things to you who believe in the name of the Son of God so that you may know that you have eternal life.

I John 5:11-13 NIV

Write down your thoughts, insights and observations below.

Meditation Question: How do you know that you have eternal life?

What is God saying to you through these verses?

How will you trust and obey Jesus today?

Write a short prayer.

Key Verse

I write these things to you who believe in the name of the Son of God
so that you may know that you have eternal life.

I John 5:13

KNOWING
GOD
BIBLE STUDY

WEEK 7

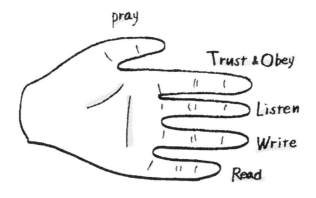

pray

Trust & Obey

Listen

Write

Read

Day 1	Romans 1
Day 2	Romans 2
Day 3	Romans 3
Day 4	Romans 4
Day 5	Romans 5

Introduction to Romans

Author & Date

Paul, who was formerly known as Saul of Tarsus, wrote this letter to the Church in Rome. Before meeting Jesus, Paul was a Pharisee. He was so zealous to defend Jewish law and traditions that he persecuted the Church and put many believers into prison. Jesus appeared to Paul on the road to Damascus and called him to be His servant. Jesus appointed Paul to be an apostle to the Gentiles.

Paul had never been to Rome, but planned to travel there sometime in the future. He learned that a community of believers had been established there. He wanted to let them know that he would be visiting them. He wanted to speak to them about some issues they were facing.

Paul wrote this letter to believers in Rome in 57 or 58 A.D., probably from Corinth. Some scholars think that Paul gave the letter to a woman named Phoebe and that she carried it to Rome.

Purpose

The believers in the church at Rome were mostly "Gentiles" (non-Jews), although there were some Jewish believers among them. They had given their lives to Jesus Christ and rejoiced in their faith in Him. At some point, however, some Jewish teachers told them that they not only had to believe in Jesus, but were required to keep the Old Testament law and observe Jewish customs. Both Jewish and Gentile believers had many questions about these teachings.

Paul wrote to the believers in Rome to answer these questions. He explained that the purpose of the Law is to expose sin. It is not a means of earning salvation. We are saved by God's grace alone, whether we are Jews or Gentiles, and this by faith. No one can earn salvation by doing works of the Law.

There were also differing opinions about whether non-Jews should keep that Sabbath, eat only kosher food, or be circumcised. Understandably both Jewish and Gentile Christians had questions related to these issues. *"Are all people really lost?" "How can I become righteous?" "Do the Old and New Testaments agree about how to be saved?" "How should I relate to people who have different opinions on these matters?" "What is the relationship of Israel to the Church today?"*

Paul dealt with these questions by clearly and systematically explaining the gospel to his readers. His focus was on righteousness through faith in Christ. Paul's main theme and purpose for writing Romans is found in chapter 1:16-17:

> [16]I am not ashamed of the gospel, because it is the power of God for the salvation of everyone who believes: first for the Jew, then for the Gentile. [17]For in the gospel a righteousness from God is revealed, a righteousness that is by faith from first to last, just as it is written: "The righteous will live by faith." NIV

Paul wanted to make it very clear that we are saved by faith in Christ and live by faith in Him.

Near the end of the letter Paul also told them that he wanted to visit them. Paul wanted to travel to Rome and then eventually go to regions beyond where the gospel had not yet been proclaimed. He said that he wanted to go as far as Spain.

Message and Main Points

As explained above, the central focus of Romans is righteousness through faith in Christ. He makes it very clear that all people have sinned, including both Jews and non-Jews. No one is righteous apart from Christ. Righteousness cannot be obtained by trying to keep the law. On the contrary, the law points out how sinful we are.

In spite of our sinfulness God made a way for us to become righteous by His grace through believing in Jesus. Our sins are completely forgiven by faith in His blood. We are justified by faith. This means that because of what Jesus did for us God legally declares us, "NOT GUILTY!"

The blood of Christ deals with the problem of our past sins. Through His blood God sees us as righteous before Him. Another problem, however, is the problem of our sin nature. Paul also explains how we are made righteous on the inside through faith in Christ. We are made one with Jesus when we believe in Him. Baptism is a symbol of becoming one with Jesus in His death and resurrection.

God is not trying to reform the old nature, but to kill it through the death of Christ. He wants us to die to the old sin nature and to live by our new nature in Christ. We can live righteously, not by striving to keep the law, but by trusting Christ to live in us. We receive His righteousness by receiving His life. He has given us the Holy Spirit to live in us so that we can live righteously and victoriously by faith in Him.

In chapters 9-11 Paul discussed the relationship of Israel to God and to the Church. Paul loved Israel and wanted them to be saved by believing in Jesus. The Gentiles received true righteousness by believing in Jesus. The Jews, however, did not attain true righteousness because they tried to become righteous by their own works. They did not have faith, but strove to establish their own righteousness.

> 30What then shall we say? That the Gentiles, who did not pursue righteousness, have obtained it, a righteousness that is by faith; 31but Israel, who pursued a law of righteousness, has not attained it. 32Why not? Because <u>they pursued it not by faith</u> but as if it were by works. Romans 9:30-32 NIV

Paul continued his emphasis on salvation by faith in his discussion of the Jewish nation. He said in chapter 10 that *"Everyone who calls on the name of the Lord will be saved."* This is not hard. It does not require super-human effort on our part to become righteous through our performance. The key is to simply believe in your heart and to confess with your mouth that Jesus is Lord whether Jew or Gentile!

For the time being Israel has been cut off from Christ like a branch cut from a tree. However, eventually they will be grafted back into Christ when they choose to believe in Him.

In chapters 12-15 Paul wrote about living out righteousness together in the Body of Christ and in society. The Body of Christ is made up of both Jews and Gentiles. We must love and forgive one another. Every member of the body has been given spiritual gifts. We love other members by using the gifts we have been given to serve one another by faith. If you love others you are fulfilling the righteous requirements of the law.

Love means to accept people who have different ideas and practices than you have. Some people observed the Sabbath (probably Jewish believers) and did not eat certain foods and meat that was sacrificed to idols. Paul taught that within the Body of Christ we must respect, accept and love others who have different views about such matters.

Paul concluded the letter by telling them about his plans to visit them in Rome and to share the gospel in regions beyond. In the last chapter Paul greeted at least 26 brothers and sisters he knew who were in Rome.

How to read Romans

Volumes of books and thousands of pages have been written about Paul's letter to believers in Rome. There is much gold to mine in each chapter. However, it is easy to be overwhelmed by the depth of these truths Paul wrote about and not grasp what he wanted every believer to understand and experience. Please do not let this happen to you. Seek not just to analyze and understand the truths in Romans intellectually, **but believe that they apply to you!**

Paul emphasized in verses 1:16-17 that the righteousness of God is revealed from faith to faith. Then he quoted the famous words from Habakkuk 2:4, *"The just will live by faith."* **Romans is a book about living by faith!** Respond to the Scriptures in faith. Chapters 1-8 contain many promises and explanations of what God has done for us in Christ. **Believe that what is written is also true of you in Christ!**

Outline of Romans: Righteous People Live by Faith.

Introduction: The righteousness of God is a gift received by faith in Christ.   1:1-7

The gospel reveals God's righteousness through faith. The righteous will

live by faith.

I.   **Mankind's Unrighteousness:** "There is none righteous, not even one!"   1-3

II.   **God's Gift of Righteousness by Faith:** "You have been declared   4-5

 not guilty because of Jesus' blood!" (You are justified by grace through

faith and are free from the penalty of past sins.)

III.   Living in Righteousness is Possible by Faith: "You have been made   6-8

one with Christ." (You are free from the power of the sin nature by the

indwelling presence of the Holy Spirit.)

IV.   **God's Righteousness and Israel:** "Israel pursued righteousness by   9-11

keeping the law." (The Gentiles received God's righteousness by faith, but

the Jewish nation rejected it.)

V.   **Practical Righteousness:** "Offer your bodies as a living sacrifice. Love   12-15

and serve others."   (Live out righteousness together in the Body of Christ and

in society.)

VI.   **Sharing Righteousness:** "My ambition is to preach the gospel where   16

Christ is not known so that all nations might believe and obey Him." (Paul's

plans and greetings.)

Hear the Word of the Lord Today!

But now a righteousness from God, apart from law, has been made known,

to which the Law and the Prophets testify. ²²This righteousness from God

comes through faith in Jesus Christ to all who believe. There is no difference,

²³for all have sinned and fall short of the glory of God, ²⁴and are justified

freely by his grace through the redemption that came by Christ Jesus.

Romans 3:21-24 NIV

The focus of the entire Bible is on Jesus. He came to redeem us from sin by grace and to set us free from the penalty of sin. Everyone who believes in Jesus is made righteous by His blood. The Law and the Prophets testify of this! We are not made righteous by keeping the Law, but by believing Jesus.

Praise God that He has made us righteous by grace through faith in Christ. Paul's letter to believers in Rome explains this truth in detail, but the whole Bible confirms it. May God give you deep understanding of your righteousness in Christ and of the tremendous blessings given to us through His amazing grace.

Week 7, Day 1

Read Romans Chapter 1. Focus on Romans 1:16-17.

Read Romans 1. Then focus on verses 1:16-17. Read these verses two or three times. Ask God to help you understand and to speak to your heart.

16 For I am not ashamed of the Good News of Christ, because it is the power of God for salvation for everyone who believes, for the Jew first, and also for the Greek. 17 For in it is revealed God's righteousness from faith to faith. As it is written, "But the righteous shall live by faith."

Romans 1:16-17

Write down your thoughts, insights and observations below.

Meditation Question: What does it mean to live by faith?

What is God saying to you through these verses?

How will you trust and obey Jesus today?

Write a short prayer.

Key Verse

"The righteous shall live by faith."

Romans 1:17

WEEK 7, DAY 2

Read Romans Chapter 2. Focus on Romans 2:28-29.

Read Romans 2. Then focus on verses 2:28-29. Read these verses two or three times. Ask God to help you understand and to speak to your heart.

28 For he is not a Jew who is one outwardly, neither is that circumcision which is outward in the flesh; 29 but he is a Jew who is one inwardly, and circumcision is that of the heart, in the spirit not in the letter; whose praise is not from men, but from God.

Romans 2:28-29

Write down your thoughts, insights and observations below.
Meditation Question: From these verses how would you describe the differences between a person who truly believes in God from someone who does not?

What is God saying to you through these verses?

How will you trust and obey Jesus today?

Write a short prayer.

Key Verse

He is a Jew who is one inwardly, and circumcision is that of the heart, in the spirit not in the letter; whose praise is not from men, but from God.

Romans 2:29

WEEK 7, DAY 3

Read Romans Chapter 3. Focus on Romans 3:9-20.

Read Romans 3. Then focus on verses 3:9-20. Read these verses two or three times. Ask God to help you understand and to speak to your heart.

⁹ What then? Are we better than they? No, in no way. For we previously warned both Jews and Greeks that they are all under sin. ¹⁰ As it is written, "There is no one righteous; no, not one. ¹¹ There is no one who understands. There is no one who seeks after God. ¹² They have all turned away. They have together become unprofitable. There is no one who does good, no, not so much as one." ¹³ "Their throat is an open tomb. With their tongues they have used deceit." "The poison of vipers is under their lips." ¹⁴ "Their mouth is full of cursing and bitterness." ¹⁵ "Their feet are swift to shed blood. ¹⁶ Destruction and misery are in their ways. ¹⁷ The way of peace, they haven't known." ¹⁸ "There is no fear of God before their eyes." ¹⁹ Now we know that whatever things the law says, it speaks to those who are under the law, that every mouth may be closed, and all the world may be brought under the judgment of God. ²⁰ Because by the works of the law, no flesh will be justified in his sight; for through the law comes the knowledge of sin. Romans 3:9-20

Write down your thoughts, insights and observations below.
Meditation Question: Describe the sinful condition of mankind from these verses.

What is God saying to you through these verses?

How will you trust and obey Jesus today?

Write a short prayer.

Key Verse

There is no one righteous; no, not one.

Romans 3:10

WEEK 7, DAY 4

Read Romans Chapter 4. Focus on Romans 4:18-21.

Read Romans 4. Then focus on verses 4:18-21. Read these verses two or three times. Ask God to help you understand and to speak to your heart.

¹⁸ Besides hope, Abraham in hope believed, to the end that he might become a father of many nations, according to that which had been spoken, "So will your offspring be." ¹⁹ Without being weakened in faith, he didn't consider his own body, already having been worn out, (he being about a hundred years old), and the deadness of Sarah's womb. ²⁰ Yet, looking to the promise of God, he didn't waver through unbelief, but grew strong through faith, giving glory to God, ²¹ and being fully assured that what he had promised, he was also able to perform.

Romans 4:18-21

Write down your thoughts, insights and observations below.
Meditation Question: What did God promise to Abraham? Why did it seem so impossible? How did Abraham believe in spite of the circumstances?

What is God saying to you through these verses?

How will you trust and obey Jesus today?

Write a short prayer.

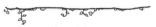

Key Verse
Yet, looking to the promise of God, he didn't waver through unbelief, but grew strong through faith, giving glory to God, and being fully assured that what he had promised, he was also able to perform.
Romans 4:20-21

WEEK 7, DAY 5

Read Romans Chapter 5. Focus on Romans 5:1-10.

Read Romans chapter 5. Then focus on verses 5:1-10. Read these verses two or three times. Ask God to help you understand and to speak to your heart.

¹ Being therefore justified by faith, we have peace with God through our Lord Jesus Christ; ² through whom we also have our access by faith into this grace in which we stand. We rejoice in hope of the glory of God. ³ Not only this, but we also rejoice in our sufferings, knowing that suffering produces perseverance; ⁴ and perseverance, proven character; and proven character, hope: ⁵ and hope doesn't disappoint us, because God's love has been poured into our hearts through the Holy Spirit who was given to us.

⁶ For while we were yet weak, at the right time Christ died for the ungodly. ⁷ For one will hardly die for a righteous man. Yet perhaps for a righteous person someone would even dare to die. ⁸ But God commends his own love toward us, in that while we were yet sinners, Christ died for us.

⁹ Much more then, being now justified by his blood, we will be saved from God's wrath through him. ¹⁰ For if while we were enemies, we were reconciled to God through the death of his Son, much more, being reconciled, we will be saved by his life. Romans 5:1-10

Write down your thoughts, insights and observations below.

Meditation Question: What blessings have been given to us in Christ?

What is God saying to you through these verses?

How will you trust and obey Jesus today?

Write a short prayer.

Key Verse

But God commends his own love toward us, in that

while we were yet sinners, Christ died for us.

Romans 5:8

KNOWING GOD

BIBLE STUDY

WEEK 8

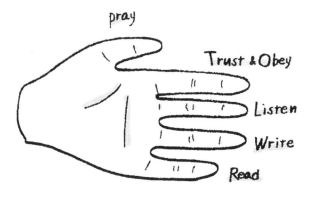

DAY 1	ROMANS 6
DAY 2	ROMANS 7
DAY 3	ROMANS 8
DAY 4	ROMANS 9
DAY 5	ROMANS 10

Hear the Word of the Lord Today!

8But what does it say? "The word is near you; it is in your mouth and in your heart," that is, the word of faith we are proclaiming: 9That if you confess with your mouth, "Jesus is Lord," and believe in your heart that God raised him from the dead, you will be saved. 10For it is with your heart that you believe and are justified, and it is with your mouth that you confess and are saved.
Romans 10:8-10

Consequently, faith comes from hearing the message, and the message is heard through the word of Christ.
Romans 10:17

Many people think that the Word of God is too hard or impossible to follow. Some think that it is only for famous preachers or special people. However, in Romans 10:8-10, Paul quoted the words of Moses (Deuteronomy 30:11-16), which says, *"The word is near! It is in your mouth and in your heart. It is the word of faith!"* God expects us to respond to Him in faith.

He does not expect us to be righteous or to perfectly keep the law in our own strength. He expects us to believe Him. Anyone can do this! Faith comes from hearing the words God speaks to you. He produces faith in us, but we must listen to Him. His words are very near! They are in your mouth and in your heart! When God speaks to us we need to respond by trusting Him. Only when we believe Him can we truly obey Him.

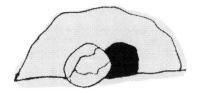

WEEK 8, DAY 1

Read Romans Chapter 6. Focus on Romans 6:22-23.

Read Romans chapter 6. Then focus on verses 6:22-23. Read these verses two or three times. Ask God to help you understand and to speak to your heart.

22 But now that you have been set free from sin and have become slaves to God, the benefit you reap leads to holiness, and the result is eternal life. 23 For the wages of sin is death, but the gift of God is eternal life in Christ Jesus our Lord.

Romans 6:22-23 NIV

Write down your thoughts, insights and observations below.

Meditation Question: How has the gift of God in Christ impacted your life?

What is God saying to you through these verses?

How will you trust and obey Jesus today?

Write a short prayer.

Key Verse

The wages of sin is death, but the gift of God is eternal life in Christ Jesus our Lord.

Romans 6:23

WEEK 8, DAY 2

Read Romans Chapter 7. Focus on Romans 7:14-20.

Read Romans 7. Then focus on verses 7:14-20. Read these verses two or three times. Ask God to help you understand and to speak to your heart.

14 We know that the law is spiritual; but I am unspiritual, sold as a slave to sin. 15 I do not understand what I do. For what I want to do I do not do, but what I hate I do. 16 And if I do what I do not want to do, I agree that the law is good. 17 As it is, it is no longer I myself who do it, but it is sin living in me. 18 I know that nothing good lives in me, that is, in my sinful nature. For I have the desire to do what is good, but I cannot carry it out. 19 For what I do is not the good I want to do; no, the evil I do not want to do—this I keep on doing. 20 Now if I do what I do not want to do, it is no longer I who do it, but it is sin living in me that does it.

Romans 7:14-20 NIV

Write down your thoughts, insights and observations below.
Meditation Question: Have you ever felt frustration like Paul expressed in these verses? What is the core problem?

What is God saying to you through these verses?

How will you trust and obey Jesus today?

Write a short prayer.

Key Verse
I do not understand what I do.
For what I want to do I do not do, but what I hate I do.
Romans 7:15

WEEK 8, DAY 3

Read Romans Chapter 8. Focus on Romans 8:1-8.

Read Romans 8. Then focus on verses 8:1-8. Read these verses two or three times. Ask God to help you understand and to speak to your heart.

[1] Therefore, there is now no condemnation for those who are in Christ Jesus, [2] because through Christ Jesus the law of the Spirit of life set me free from the law of sin and death. [3] For what the law was powerless to do in that it was weakened by the sinful nature, God did by sending his own Son in the likeness of sinful man to be a sin offering. And so he condemned sin in sinful man, [4] in order that the righteous requirements of the law might be fully met in us, who do not live according to the sinful nature but according to the Spirit. [5] Those who live according to the sinful nature have their minds set on what that nature desires; but those who live in accordance with the Spirit have their minds set on what the Spirit desires. [6] The mind of sinful man is death, but the mind controlled by the Spirit is life and peace; [7] the sinful mind is hostile to God. It does not submit to God's law, nor can it do so. [8] Those controlled by the sinful nature cannot please God.
Romans 8:1-8 NIV

Write down your thoughts, insights and observations below.
Meditation Question: What did you learn from these verses about living according to the sin nature compared to living according to the Spirit?

What is God saying to you through these verses?

How will you trust and obey Jesus today?

Write a short prayer.

Key Verse

The mind of sinful man is death, but the mind controlled by the Spirit is life and peace.

Romans 8:6

Week 8, Day 4

Read Romans Chapter 9. Focus on Romans 9:30-33.

📖 **Read Romans 9. Then focus on verses 9:30-33. Read these verses two or three times. Ask God to help you understand and to speak to your heart.**

³⁰ What then shall we say? That the Gentiles, who did not pursue righteousness, have obtained it, a righteousness that is by faith; ³¹ but Israel, who pursued a law of righteousness, has not attained it. ³² Why not? Because they pursued it not by faith but as if it were by works. They stumbled over the "stumbling stone." ³³ As it is written:

"See, I lay in Zion a stone that causes men to stumble and a rock that makes them fall, and the one who trusts in him will never be put to shame."

Romans 9:30-33 NIV

📖 **Write down your thoughts, insights and observations below.**
Meditation Question: How did the gentiles obtain righteousness? Why did Israel not attain righteousness?

💬 **What is God saying to you through these verses?**

✝ **How will you trust and obey Jesus today?**

🙏 **Write a short prayer.**

Key Verse

³⁰The Gentiles, who did not pursue righteousness, have obtained it, a righteousness that is by faith; ³¹but Israel, who pursued a law of righteousness, has not attained it. ³²Why not? Because they pursued it not by faith but as if it were by works.

Romans 9:30-32

WEEK 8, DAY 5

Read Romans Chapter 10. Focus on Romans 10:8-11.

Read Romans 10. Then focus on verses 10:8-11. Read these verses two or three times. Ask God to help you understand and to speak to your heart.

[8] But what does it say? "The word is near you; it is in your mouth and in your heart," that is, the word of faith we are proclaiming: [9] That if you confess with your mouth, "Jesus is Lord," and believe in your heart that God raised him from the dead, you will be saved. [10] For it is with your heart that you believe and are justified, and it is with your mouth that you confess and are saved. [11] As the Scripture says, "Anyone who trusts in him will never be put to shame."

Romans 10:8-11 NIV

Write down your thoughts, insights and observations below.
Meditation Question: What is the role of your heart and your mouth in expressing faith?

What is God saying to you through these verses?

How will you trust and obey Jesus today?

Write a short prayer.

Key Verse

If you confess with your mouth, "Jesus is Lord," and believe in your
heart that God raised him from the dead, you will be saved.

Romans 10:9

KNOWING
GOD
BIBLE STUDY

Week 9

Day 1   Romans 11

Day 2   Romans 12

Day 3   Romans 13

Day 4   Romans 14

Day 5   Romans 15

HEAR THE WORD OF THE LORD TODAY!

⁸ Owe no one anything, except to love one another; for he who loves his neighbor has fulfilled the law. ⁹ For the commandments, "You shall not commit adultery," "You shall not murder," "You shall not steal," "You shall not covet," and whatever other commandments are all summed up in this saying, namely, "You shall love your neighbor as yourself." ¹⁰ Love doesn't harm a neighbor. Love therefore is the fulfillment of the law. Romans 13:8-10

God is love. The greatest command is to love the Lord with all of our heart, soul and mind. The second greatest command is to love our neighbor as ourselves. If we truly love others, it means that we are fulfilling the law. The whole Law is summed up in this one command: "Love your neighbor as yourself." We are living according to God's design when we love others. May your study of the Bible lead you to love others more and more this week!

WEEK 9, DAY 1

Read Romans Chapter 11. Focus on Romans 11:33-36.

Read Romans 11. Then focus on verses 11:33-36. Read these verses two or three times. Ask God to help you understand and to speak to your heart.

33 Oh the depth of the riches both of the wisdom and the knowledge of God!

How unsearchable are his judgments, and his ways past finding out!

34 "For who has known the mind of the Lord? Or who has been his counselor?"

35 "Or who has first given to him, and has to be repaid?"

36 For of him, and through him, and to him are all things.

To him be the glory for ever! Amen.

Romans 11:33-36

Write down your thoughts, insights and observations below.
Meditation Question: What did you learn about the greatness of God from these verses?

What is God saying to you through these verses?

How will you trust and obey Jesus today?

Write a short prayer.

Key Verse

For of him, and through him, and to him are all things.

To him be the glory for ever! Amen.

Romans 11:36

Week 9, Day 2

Read Romans Chapter 12. Focus on Romans 12:14-21.

 **Read Romans 12. Then focus on verses 12:14-21. Read these verses two or three times. Ask God to help you understand and to speak to your heart.**

¹⁴ Bless those who persecute you; bless and do not curse. ¹⁵ Rejoice with those who rejoice; mourn with those who mourn. ¹⁶ Live in harmony with one another. Do not be proud, but be willing to associate with people of low position. Do not be conceited.¹⁷ Do not repay anyone evil for evil. Be careful to do what is right in the eyes of everybody. ¹⁸ If it is possible, as far as it depends on you, live at peace with everyone. ¹⁹ Do not take revenge, my friends, but leave room for God's wrath, for it is written: "It is mine to avenge; I will repay," says the Lord. ²⁰ On the contrary:
"If your enemy is hungry, feed him if he is thirsty, give him something to drink.
In doing this, you will heap burning coals on his head." ²¹ Do not be overcome
by evil, but overcome evil with good.
Romans 12:14-21 NIV

 **Write down your thoughts, insights and observations below.**

Meditation Question: How can we overcome evil with good?

 **What is God saying to you through these verses?**

✝ **How will you trust and obey Jesus today?**

Write a short prayer.

Key Verse

Do not be overcome by evil, but overcome evil with good.

Romans 12:21

WEEK 9, DAY 3

Read Romans Chapter 13. Focus on Romans 13:8-10.

Read Romans 13. Then focus on verses 13:8-10. Read these verses two or three times. Ask God to help you understand and to speak to your heart.

⁸ Owe no one anything, except to love one another; for he who loves his neighbor has fulfilled the law. ⁹ For the commandments, "You shall not commit adultery," "You shall not murder," "You shall not steal," "You shall not covet," and whatever other commandments there are, are all summed up in this saying, namely, "You shall love your neighbor as yourself." ¹⁰ Love doesn't harm a neighbor. Love therefore is the fulfillment of the law.

Romans 13:8-10

Write down your thoughts, insights and observations below.
Meditation Question: How does the command to, "Love your neighbor as yourself," fulfill every commandment in God's law?

What is God saying to you through these verses?

How will you trust and obey Jesus today?

Write a short prayer.

Key Verse

Owe no one anything, except to love one another;

for he who loves his neighbor has fulfilled the law.

Romans 13:8

WEEK 9, DAY 4

Read Romans Chapter 14. Focus on Romans 14:1-4.

Read Romans 14. Then focus on verses 14:1-4. Read these verses two or three times. Ask God to help you understand and to speak to your heart.

1 Accept him whose faith is weak, without passing judgment on disputable matters. 2 One man's faith allows him to eat everything, but another man, whose faith is weak, eats only vegetables. 3 The man who eats everything must not look down on him who does not, and the man who does not eat everything must not condemn the man who does, for God has accepted him. 4 Who are you to judge someone else's servant? To his own master he stands or falls. And he will stand, for the Lord is able to make him stand.

Romans 14:1-4 NIV

Write down your thoughts, insights and observations below.
Meditation Question: Do you judge others sometimes? Whose job is it to judge?

What is God saying to you through these verses?

How will you trust and obey Jesus today?

Write a short prayer.

Key Verse

Accept him whose faith is weak, without passing judgment on disputable matters.

Romans 14:1

WEEK 9, DAY 5

Read Romans Chapter 15. Focus on Romans 15:5-7.

Read Romans 15. Then focus on verses 15:5-7. Read these verses two or three times. Ask God to help you understand and to speak to your heart.

⁵May the God who gives endurance and encouragement give you a spirit of unity among yourselves as you follow Christ Jesus, ⁶so that with one heart and mouth you may glorify the God and Father of our Lord Jesus Christ. ⁷Accept one another, then, just as Christ accepted you, in order to bring praise to God.

Romans 15:5-7 NIV

Write down your thoughts, insights and observations below.
Meditation Question: According to these verses what kind of relationship does God want you to have with others in your fellowship?

What is God saying to you through these verses?

How will you trust and obey Jesus today?

Write a short prayer.

Key Verse
Accept one another, then, just as Christ accepted you,
in order to bring praise to God.
Romans 15:7

KNOWING
GOD
BIBLE STUDY

Week 10

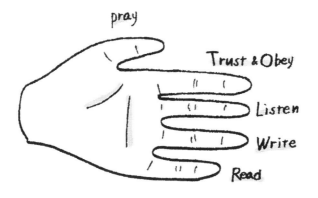

pray

Trust & Obey

Listen

Write

Read

Day 1	Romans 16
Day 2	1 Timothy 1
Day 3	1 Timothy 2
Day 4	1 Timothy 3
Day 5	1 Timothy 4

Introduction to I Timothy

The letters to Timothy along with Titus are called the "Pastoral Epistles." However, this name may be misleading. Timothy and Titus were not really called to pastoral ministry. They were a part of Paul's apostolic team. They were sent to establish churches on a good foundation, to deal with problems like false teachers, and to appoint elders and deacons who would continue leading the churches after Timothy and Titus moved on.

More than being pastors or evangelists Timothy and Titus functioned as apostles. It seems clear that in every area there was not a one-person hierarchical leadership structure, but a plurality of leaders. There were teams of apostles, elders and deacons.

Author & Date

Most conservative scholars agree that I Timothy was written by the Apostle Paul to Timothy sometime after 64 A.D. Paul referred to Timothy as his spiritual son. Timothy accompanied Paul on his second and third missionary journeys and they had a very close relationship.

Paul and Barnabas had shared the gospel in Lystra on one of their missionary journeys. It is likely that a Jewish woman named Lois and her daughter Eunice believed in Christ at that time. Eunice was married to a Gentile and Timothy was their son. The father probably refused to allow Timothy to be circumcised. On his second visit to Lystra Paul added Timothy to his apostolic team. Since they would be sharing with Jewish people as well as with Gentiles, Paul urged Timothy to be circumcised to avoid offending the Jews because Timothy's mother was Jewish.

Paul visited Ephesus in A.D. 63. It is thought that when Paul left Ephesus he left Timothy there to continue the ministry. Paul wrote his first letter to Timothy around 64 A.D.

Purpose

Paul wrote to Timothy to encourage him and to instruct him about the ministry he was doing. Timothy had to deal with false teachers, false doctrines and an assortment of other problems. Paul gave instruction to Timothy about worship, qualifications for elders and deacons, the importance of godliness, taking care of widows, and one's attitude and use of money.

Message and Main Points

The task Timothy was given to guide the church in his area had many challenges. Timothy was told to confront false teachers and to teach sound doctrine. Paul laid out the qualifications for leadership and told Timothy to choose elders and deacons based on their life and character. Paul urged Timothy to be godly in his lifestyle and to be an example to all believers.

Paul gave Timothy guidelines for supporting widows. He also told him how to treat elders and leaders in the church. He warned Timothy that the love of money is the root of all kinds of evil and that those who want to be rich fall into temptation that has caused many to fall away from the faith. Paul charged Timothy to pursue righteousness and to fight the good fight of faith. He told Timothy to teach rich people not to be proud or to trust in their wealth, but to do good and to be rich in good works.

Outline of I Timothy

Paul's Instructions to His Spiritual Son: Persevere and Continue Apostolic Ministry

Hear the Word of the Lord Today!

The goal of this command is love, which comes from a pure heart

and a good conscience and a sincere faith.

I Timothy 1:5

God is love and His main command is to love one another. This is the goal of the Bible, that we walk in love. He wants us to have true love that comes from a pure heart. True love does not have mixed motives. We must love people unconditionally, not because we want to get something from them. A good conscience means that we have no voice inside telling us that we have wronged someone else or have been unloving towards them. This love comes from a sincere faith. It means that we are truly trusting God with our lives and believing Him to flow His love through us. May God fill you with His love and with His presence every day as you walk in love.

Week 10, Day 1

Read Romans Chapter 16. Focus on Romans 16:25-27.

Read Romans 16. Then focus on verses 16:25-27. Read these verses two or three times. Ask God to help you understand and to speak to your heart.

25 Now to him who is able to establish you by my gospel and the proclamation of Jesus Christ, according to the revelation of the mystery hidden for long ages past, 26 but now revealed and made known through the prophetic writings by the command of the eternal God, so that all nations might believe and obey him— 27 to the only wise God be glory forever through Jesus Christ! Amen.

Romans 16:25-27 NIV

Write down your thoughts, insights and observations below.

Meditation Question: Why did God reveal this mystery?

What is God saying to you through these verses?

How will you trust and obey Jesus today?

Write a short prayer.

Key Verse

To the only wise God be glory forever through Jesus Christ! Amen.

Romans 16:27

Week 10, Day 2

Read 1 Timothy Chapter 1. Focus on 1 Timothy 1:12-17.

Read 1 Timothy 1. Then focus on verses 1:12-17. Read these verses two or three times. Ask God to help you understand and to speak to your heart.

[12] I thank Christ Jesus our Lord, who has given me strength, that he considered me faithful, appointing me to his service. [13] Even though I was once a blasphemer and a persecutor and a violent man, I was shown mercy because I acted in ignorance and unbelief. [14] The grace of our Lord was poured out on me abundantly, along with the faith and love that are in Christ Jesus. [15] Here is a trustworthy saying that deserves full acceptance: Christ Jesus came into the world to save sinners—of whom I am the worst. [16] But for that very reason I was shown mercy so that in me, the worst of sinners, Christ Jesus might display his unlimited patience as an example for those who would believe on him and receive eternal life. [17] Now to the King eternal, immortal, invisible, the only God, be honor and glory for ever and ever. Amen. I Timothy 1:12-17 NIV

Write down your thoughts, insights and observations below.

Meditation Question: How did Paul experience the mercy of God?

What is God saying to you through these verses?

How will you trust and obey Jesus today?

Write a short prayer.

Key Verse

Now to the King eternal, immortal, invisible, the only God, be honor

and glory for ever and ever. Amen.

I Timothy 1:17

Week 10, Day 3

Read I Timothy Chapter 2. Focus on I Timothy 2:1-6.

Read 1 Timothy 2. Then focus on verses 2:1-6. Read these verses two or three times. Ask God to help you understand and to speak to your heart.

[1]I urge, then, first of all, that requests, prayers, intercession and thanksgiving be made for everyone—[2]for kings and all those in authority, that we may live peaceful and quiet lives in all godliness and holiness. [3]This is good, and pleases God our Savior, [4]who wants all men to be saved and to come to a knowledge of the truth. [5]For there is one God and one mediator between God and men, the man Christ Jesus, [6]who gave himself as a ransom for all men—the testimony given in its proper time.

I Timothy 2:1-6 NIV

Write down your thoughts, insights and observations below.
    Meditation Question: Who should we pray for? What do these verses teach about Jesus?

What is God saying to you through these verses?

How will you trust and obey Jesus today?

Write a short prayer.

Key Verse
For there is one God and one mediator between God and men,
the man Christ Jesus.
I Timothy 2:5

WEEK 10, DAY 4

Read I Timothy Chapter 3. Focus on I Timothy 3:13.

Read 1 Timothy 3. Then focus on verses 3:13. Read these verses two or three times. Ask God to help you understand and to speak to your heart.

> Those who have served well gain an excellent standing and
> great assurance in their faith in Christ Jesus.
> I Timothy 3:13 NIV

Write down your thoughts, insights and observations below.
Meditation Question: If we serve others well what will be the result? Who do you think God wants you to serve?

What is God saying to you through these verses?

How will you trust and obey Jesus today?

Write a short prayer.

Key Verse
Those who have served well gain an excellent standing and
great assurance in their faith in Christ Jesus.
I Timothy 3:13

Week 10, Day 5

Read I Timothy Chapter 4. Focus on I Timothy 4:8.

Read 1 Timothy 4. Then focus on verses 4:8. Read these verses two or three times. Ask God to help you understand and to speak to your heart.

> For physical training is of some value, but godliness has value for all things,
>
> holding promise for both the present life and the life to come.
>
> I Timothy 4:8 NIV

Write down your thoughts, insights and observations below.
Meditation Question: Do you exercise or do physical training? What about spiritual training? What is your plan for growing spiritually?

What is God saying to you through these verses?

How will you trust and obey Jesus today?

Write a short prayer.

Key Verse

For physical training is of some value, but godliness has value for all things,

holding promise for both the present life and the life to come.

I Timothy 4:8

KNOWING GOD

BIBLE STUDY

Week 11

pray

Trust & Obey

Listen

Write

Read

Day 1	1 Timothy 5
Day 2	1 Timothy 6
Day 3	2 John
Day 4	3 John
Day 5	Ephesians 1

Introduction to II John

Author & Date

The author of both II John and III John identifies himself as *"the elder."* He was the apostle John, the Son of Zebedee. In the Gospel of John he called himself, *"the disciple whom Jesus loved."* At this time John probably lived near Ephesus. John the Apostle probably wrote this second letter around 90 A.D.

The letter is addressed to, *"the chosen lady and her children."* This could refer to a specific woman and her children. However, some scholars think that it refers to a local church and its members. This author thinks that John was writing to a mother who was a close friend. If so this is the only letter in the New Testament written to a woman.

Purpose

During the first century traveling evangelists and teachers went from place to place teaching the churches and sharing the gospel. Believers in each location took them in and gave them provisions when they departed. False teachers also traveled from place to place and stayed in people's homes. In this letter John urged his readers to discern whether or not their teaching is really from God. He told them not to welcome or support people who were spreading false teachings.

Message and Main Points

In verse 4 John wrote, *"It has given me great joy to find some of your children walking in the truth, just as the Father commanded us."* John had met some children of the Lady he was writing to who were walking in love so he knew that they were walking in truth. John challenged them, as in his other letters to love one another. This is how we follow Christ and walk in truth. If we love one another we are walking according to God's commandments.

John also emphasized that love must be discerning. Walking in love does not mean to naively receive anyone no matter what they say or do. We must walk in love, but also walk in truth. Sometimes this means to not receive people who are not walking in truth.

A common denominator of most cults is that they deny Christ in some way. Most deny that he is God. The Gnostic heresy in the first century talked about Jesus. However, they said that he did not really come in the flesh, but only in spirit. John said in verse 7 that, *"Many deceivers have gone out into the world; they do not confess the coming of Jesus Christ in the flesh. This is the deceiver and the antichrist."* John could have been referring to Gnostic teachers. He went on to say that if a person does not remain in the basic teaching about Christ they do not have God. However, if they remain in the teaching about Christ, they have both the Father and the Son.

Outline of II John

Introduction to III John

Author & Date

John the Apostle wrote this letter to a friend named Gaius, probably around A.D. 90. John had heard about problems in their network of house churches. Gaius was hospitable and he welcomed traveling co-workers, but a man named Diotrephes was hostile and rejected them. Diotrephes was selfish and wanted to be in control. John wrote to his friend Gaius about this situation.

Purpose

John wrote to commend Gaius for his love and faithful service. He welcomed brothers who were travelling co-workers and provided for them. John rebuked Diotrephes for his selfishness and refusal to welcome brothers and co-workers. John also wrote to affirm Demetrius whose life was a good testimony to John and to others.

Message and Main Points

John said in verse 4, *"I have no greater joy than to know that my children walk in truth."* He said in verse 3 that Gaius was walking in the truth. Thus Gaius may have been one of John's disciples, a spiritual son in the Lord. It is a great joy to see both our physical children and spiritual children walking in truth and following Christ with their whole heart. And it is very troubling when our children do not walk in truth and do not follow Christ.

Paul encouraged Gaius to continue to welcome and support traveling co-workers. Gaius had a good reputation for showing hospitality to traveling co-workers and for showing practical love. This was evidence that he was walking in truth.

Diotrephes, however, was not walking in love. He wanted to be first and to be in control. He attacked others with slanderous and malicious words. He refused to welcome co-workers and stopped those who did welcome them. He even put some of them out of the church. This was a complete abuse of authority and a contradiction of the main command, which is to love others.

John made a statement by which we can evaluate Diotrephes or anyone who claims to be following Christ. John said in verse 11, *"The one who does good is of God; the one who does evil has not seen God."* Somehow, Diotrephes had become a leader, but it is clear that he really did not know God. John said that everyone, including himself, spoke well of Demetrius.

Outline of III John

Hear the Word of the Lord Today!

Do not let this Book of the Law depart from your mouth; meditate on it day and night, so that you may be careful to do everything written in it. Then you will be prosperous and successful.

Joshua 1:8 NIV

This is a great promise. According to this verse you will be prosperous and successful if you meditate on God's Word day and night. This does not mean that we sit at a desk reading the Bible twenty-four hours a day. However, your daily time in the Word is the starting point. Make time to spend time with God today. Let His words flood your heart and mind. Meditate and think about His words throughout the day. He will make you prosperous and successful!

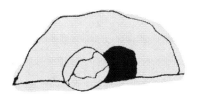

Week 11, Day 1

Read I Timothy Chapter 5. Focus on I Timothy 5:1-2.

Read 1 Timothy 5. Then focus on verses 5:1-2. Read these verses two or three times. Ask God to help you understand and to speak to your heart.

¹ Do not rebuke an older man harshly, but exhort him as if he were your father. Treat younger men as brothers, ² older women as mothers, and younger women as sisters, with absolute purity.

I Timothy 5:1-2 NIV

Write down your thoughts, insights and observations below.

Meditation Question: Summarize these verses in your own words.

What is God saying to you through these verses?

How will you trust and obey Jesus today?

Write a short prayer.

Key Verse
¹ Do not rebuke an older man harshly, but exhort him as if he were your father.
Treat younger men as brothers, ² older women as mothers, and younger women
as sisters, with absolute purity.
I Timothy 5:1-2

WEEK 11, DAY 2

Read I Timothy Chapter 6. Focus on I Timothy 6:6-10.

Read I Timothy 6. Then focus on verses 6:6-10. Read these verses two or three times. Ask God to help you understand and to speak to your heart.

⁶ But godliness with contentment is great gain. ⁷ For we brought nothing into the world, and we can take nothing out of it. ⁸ But if we have food and clothing, we will be content with that. ⁹ People who want to get rich fall into temptation and a trap and into many foolish and harmful desires that plunge men into ruin and destruction. ¹⁰ For the love of money is a root of all kinds of evil. Some people, eager for money, have wandered from the faith and pierced themselves with many griefs.

I Timothy 6:6-10 NIV

Write down your thoughts, insights and observations below.

Meditation Question: Why should we be content with food and clothing?

What is God saying to you through these verses?

How will you trust and obey Jesus today?

Write a short prayer.

Key Verse

For the love of money is a root of all kinds of evil.

I Timothy 6:10

Week 11, Day 3

Read II John 1. Focus on II John 1:6.

Read II John chapter 1. Then focus on verse 1:6. Read these verses two or three times. Ask God to help you understand and to speak to your heart.

And this is love: that we walk in obedience to his commands. As you have heard from the
beginning, his command is that you walk in love.

II John 1:6 NIV

Write down your thoughts, insights and observations below.
Meditation Question: Do you think that if we love others we will be obeying
all of the commands God wants us to obey? Explain your answer.

What is God saying to you through these verses?

How will you trust and obey Jesus today?

Write a short prayer.

Key Verse

And this is love: that we walk in obedience to his commands. As you have heard from the
beginning, his command is that you walk in love.

II John 1:6

WEEK 11, DAY 4

Read III John 1. Focus on III John 1:2-4.

Read III John 1. Then focus on verses 1:2-4. Read these verses two or three times. Ask God to help you understand and to speak to your heart.

² Dear friend, I pray that you may enjoy good health and that all may go well with you, even as your soul is getting along well. ³ It gave me great joy to have some brothers come and tell about your faithfulness to the truth and how you continue to walk in the truth. ⁴ I have no greater joy than to hear that my children are walking in the truth.

III John 1:2-4 NIV

Write down your thoughts, insights and observations below.
Meditation Question: Why do people have great joy when their children or spiritual children are walking in the truth?

What is God saying to you through these verses?

How will you trust and obey Jesus today?

Write a short prayer.

Key Verse

I have no greater joy than to hear that my children are walking in the truth.

III John 1:4

Week 11, Day 5

Read Ephesians Chapter 1. Focus on Ephesians 1:3-10.

Read Ephesians 1. Then focus on verses 1:3-10. Read these verses two or three times. Ask God to help you understand and to speak to your heart.

³ Blessed be the God and Father of our Lord Jesus Christ, who has blessed us with every spiritual blessing in the heavenly places in Christ, ⁴ even as he chose us in him before the foundation of the world, that we would be holy and without defect before him in love, ⁵ having predestined us for adoption as children through Jesus Christ to himself, according to the good pleasure of his desire, ⁶ to the praise of the glory of his grace, by which he freely gave us favor in the Beloved, ⁷ in whom we have our redemption through his blood, the forgiveness of our trespasses, according to the riches of his grace, ⁸ which he made to abound toward us in all wisdom and prudence, ⁹ making known to us the mystery of his will, according to his good pleasure which he purposed in him ¹⁰ to an administration of the fullness of the times, to sum up all things in Christ, the things in the heavens and the things on the earth, in him.

Ephesians 1:3-10 NIV

Write down your thoughts, insights and observations below.

Meditation Question: List some of the blessings God has given us in Christ.

What is God saying to you through these verses?

How will you trust and obey Jesus today?

Write a short prayer.

Key Verse

Blessed be the God and Father of our Lord Jesus Christ, who has blessed us

with every spiritual blessing in the heavenly places in Christ.

Ephesians 1:3

KNOWING GOD

BIBLE STUDY

WEEK 12

pray

Trust & Obey

Listen

Write

Read

DAY 1	EPHESIANS 2
DAY 2	EPHESIANS 3
DAY 3	EPHESIANS 4
DAY 4	EPHESIANS 5
DAY 5	EPHESIANS 6

Introduction to Ephesians

Author & Date

The author identifies himself as Paul. This epistle is known as one of his Prison Letters (called epistles) because it, along with Philippians, Colossians, and Philemon was written from Rome while Paul was kept under guard in his rental quarters. This being the case, the date of writing would be around 60-61 A.D.

Ephesus was a port on the west coast of Asia minor (now Turkey) and a major commercial center. Paul went to Ephesus in the winter of A.D. 55 and stayed there for 2-3 years (Acts 19:8-10). He made Ephesus a center of evangelism and discipleship training.

Purpose

Paul does not address any particular problem in this letter. He wrote to explain God's eternal purpose and to make clear the essence and goal of the Church. Ephesians reveals the eternal purpose of God, which was a mystery, hidden until Christ appeared. God's eternal purpose is to dwell among His people. He formed both Jews and Gentiles into one new man, which is Christ's Body, the Church. His plan is to manifest His life through His Body! In the Body of Christ we can know the greatness of His love and also experience the fullness of God.

Message and Main Points

The theme of Ephesians is called God's eternal purpose. Paul explained in chapter 3 that this was a great mystery that had been hidden, but was revealed to him. The mystery is the Church, which is the Body of Christ. Christ is the Head and expresses His life through His Body. The Church is not an institution or organization. It is a living organism. The life of Christ can only be seen through people who are living in love relationship with Him. Jesus can manifest His life fully through His Body.

The first three chapters of Ephesians describe our Wealth in Christ and in His Body. They reveal the majesty and greatness of blessings made available to us in Christ. They describe our identity in Christ and the blessings that are ours in Him. He forgave our sins and adopted us as His children. He has given us the Holy Spirit and manifests His fullness through us, His Body. He has made us one in Him. He reconciled us to God and to one another. He dwells among us and reveals the fullness of His life to us and through us.

The Church is made up of people who He made into one new man in Christ. They are the Body of Christ, the Family of the Father, and the Temple of the Holy Spirit, which is the dwelling place of God. The Church is Christ incarnate! The Church is Christ expressed through His Body. Paul offers two prayers asking God to give revelation and insight so that we might know the power of Christ in us and express the fullness of His love to people around us (1:15-23 and 3:14-21).

Ephesians chapters 4:1 to 6:9 discuss our Walk with Christ in His Body. We are one Body in Him. Jesus gave apostles, prophets, pastors, teachers and evangelists to equip every member of the Body to do ministry. The result of this equipping is that we are joined to Christ the Head of the Body and to one another.

We grow to maturity as each member builds the other members of the Body up in love. As the Body of Christ we can fully express His life in our daily lives. Then we can walk in love in society, in the community of believers and in our families.

Chapter 6:10-24 describes our Warfare together with Christ and with His Body. We are engaged in a spiritual battle. He tells us to be strong in the Lord and in the power of His might. Paul instructs us to put on armor so that we may be able to stand against the spiritual powers of darkness. Various pieces of armor are given to us who are in Christ. We should not think of this battle as an individual fighting against the forces of evil by himself or by herself. We can only be victorious in this battle together, as the Body of Christ.

Outline of Ephesians

God's Eternal Purpose

I.   Our Wealth in Christ and in His Body   1-3

II. Our Walk with Christ in His Body   4:1-6:9

III. Our Warfare Together with Christ as His Body   6:10-24

Hear the Word of the Lord Today!

Take the helmet of salvation and
the sword of the Spirit, which is the word of God.
Ephesians 6:17

For **the word of God is living and active. Sharper than
any double-edged sword**, it penetrates even to dividing soul
and spirit, joints and marrow; it judges the
thoughts and attitudes of the heart.
Hebrews 4:12 NIV

The Word of God is called the sword of the Spirit. It is not just a collection of good teachings to analyze intellectually. The Word of God is living and active! It is sharp and powerful. It can penetrate into our hearts and souls. It can reveal and judge our thoughts, attitudes and motives. Hearing the word of the Lord means to let Him speak to the issues in our hearts and to let Him change us. Open your heart and hear God's words today!   Let the Sword of the Spirit penetrate your heart and soul. Then you will be able to use the sword of the Spirit to penetrate the hearts of others.

WEEK 12, DAY 1

Read Ephesians Chapter 2. Focus on Ephesians 2:8-9.

Read Ephesians 2. Then focus on verse 2:8-9. Read these verses two or three times. Ask God to help you understand and to speak to your heart.

For by grace you have been saved through faith, and that not of yourselves; it is the gift of God, not of works, so that no one can boast.

Ephesians 2:8-9 NIV

Write down your thoughts, insights and observations below.

Meditation Question: Explain why no one can boast about being saved.

What is God saying to you through these verses?

How will you trust and obey Jesus today?

Write a short prayer.

Key Verse

For by grace you have been saved through faith, and that not of yourselves;
it is the gift of God, not of works, that no one can boast.

Ephesians 2:8-9

WEEK 12, DAY 2

Read Ephesians Chapter 3. Focus on Ephesians 3:14-19.

Read Ephesians 3. Then focus on verse 3:14-19. Read these verses two or three times. Ask God to help you understand and to speak to your heart.

14 For this cause, I bow my knees to the Father of our Lord Jesus Christ, 15 from whom every family in heaven and on earth is named, 16 that he would grant you, according to the riches of his glory, that you may be strengthened with power through his Spirit in the inner person, 17 that Christ may dwell in your hearts through faith, to the end that you, being rooted and grounded in love, 18 may be strengthened to comprehend with all the saints what is the width and length and height and depth, 19 and to know Christ's love which surpasses knowledge, that you may be filled with all the fullness of God.

Ephesians 3:14-19 NIV

Write down your thoughts, insights and observations below.
Meditation Question: What are 3 or 4 things from this prayer that you can pray for others?

What is God saying to you through these verses?

How will you trust and obey Jesus today?

Write a short prayer.

Key Verse
17 That Christ may dwell in your hearts through faith, to the end that you, being rooted and grounded in love, 18 may be strengthened to comprehend with all the saints what is the width and length and height and depth, 19 and to know Christ's love which surpasses knowledge, that you may be filled with all the fullness of God.
Ephesians 3:17-19

WEEK 12, DAY 3

Read Ephesians Chapter 4. Focus on Ephesians 4:29-32.

Read Ephesians 4. Then focus on verse 4:29-32. Read these verses two or three times. Ask God to help you understand and to speak to your heart.

29 Let no corrupt speech proceed out of your mouth, but only what is good for building others up as the need may be, that it may give grace to those who hear. 30 Don't grieve the Holy Spirit of God, in whom you were sealed for the day of redemption. 31 Let all bitterness, wrath, anger, outcry, and slander be put away from you, with all malice. 32 And be kind to one another, tender hearted, forgiving each other, just as God also in Christ forgave you.

Ephesians 4:29-32 NIV

Write down your thoughts, insights and observations below.

Meditation Question: What keys to loving others can you find in these verses?

What is God saying to you through these verses?

How will you trust and obey Jesus today?

Write a short prayer.

Key Verse

And be kind to one another, tender hearted, forgiving each other,

just as God also in Christ forgave you.

Ephesians 4:32

Week 12, Day 4

Read Ephesians Chapter 5. Focus on Ephesians 5:18-21.

Read Ephesians 5. Then focus on verse 5:18-21. Read these verses two or three times. Ask God to help you understand and to speak to your heart.

¹⁸ Do not get drunk on wine, which leads to debauchery. Instead, be filled with the Spirit. ¹⁹ Speak to one another with psalms, hymns and spiritual songs. Sing and make music in your heart to the Lord, ²⁰ always giving thanks to God the Father for everything, in the name of our Lord Jesus Christ. ²¹ Submit to one another out of reverence for Christ.

Ephesians 5:18-21 NIV

Write down your thoughts, insights and observations below.
Meditation Question: According to these verses, how should being filled with the Spirit be expressed in our lives?

What is God saying to you through these verses?

How will you trust and obey Jesus today?

Write a short prayer.

Key Verse
¹⁹ Speak to one another with psalms, hymns and spiritual songs. Sing and make music in your heart to the Lord, ²⁰ always giving thanks to God the Father for everything, in the name of our Lord Jesus Christ.
Ephesians 5:19-20

Week 12, Day 5

Read Ephesians Chapter 6. Focus on Ephesians 6:10-12.

Read Ephesians 6. Then focus on verse 6:10-12. Read these verses two or three times. Ask God to help you understand and to speak to your heart.

[10] Finally, be strong in the Lord and in his mighty power. [11] Put on the full armor of God so that you can take your stand against the devil's schemes. [12] For our struggle is not against flesh and blood, but against the rulers, against the authorities, against the powers of this dark world and against the spiritual forces of evil in the heavenly realms.

Ephesians 6:10-12 NIV

Write down your thoughts, insights and observations below.
Meditation Question: Describe the battle we are in. How can we be strong in the Lord?

What is God saying to you through these verses?

How will you trust and obey Jesus today?

Write a short prayer.

Key Verse

Finally, be strong in the Lord and in his mighty power.

Ephesians 6:10

KNOWING GOD

BIBLE STUDY

WEEK 13

pray
Trust & Obey
Listen
Write
Read

Day 1	PHILEMON
Day 2	II TIMOTHY 1
Day 3	II TIMOTHY 2
Day 4	II TIMOTHY 3
Day 5	II TIMOTHY 4

Introduction to Philemon

Author & Date

Paul wrote this letter to Philemon while in prison in Rome, around A.D. 60-61. Philemon was a wealthy Roman citizen from Colossae who perhaps met Paul in Ephesus and became a follower of Jesus. Later Epaphras, Paul's co-worker, started a community of believers in Colossae. Philemon probably became a leader of the church that met in his house.

Purpose

Philemon owned slaves. One of them was named Onesimus. At some point Onesimus wronged Philemon in some way and ran away. (Perhaps he stole money or something else.) Later Onesimus met Paul who was in prison in Rome. Through this relationship Onesimus became a believer in Jesus. Paul wrote to Philemon and asked him to forgive Onesimus and to not only receive him back, but to accept him as a brother.

Message and Main Points

According to Roman law runaway slaves could be severely punished or put to death. Onesimus would never have returned to Colossae and to his master Philemon if he had not become a follower of Jesus. Paul wrote this letter to appeal to Philemon on behalf of Onesimus, who was going to return to his master.

Paul wanted to do the right thing and to reconcile Onesimus to Philemon. However, it is clear from the letter that Paul also wanted to change Philemon's core thinking. He wanted Philemon to not see Onesimus as a slave, but as a precious brother in Christ. It is of course important to change laws about such things as slavery. However, there will not be real transformation unless people change their core values and way of thinking. The goal of the gospel is to change people from the inside out.

Outline of Philemon

I.   Paul's Prayer of Thanksgiving and Blessing for Philemon   1-7

II. Paul's Appeal to Philemon for Onesimus   8-21

III. Final Greetings   22-25

Introduction to II Timothy

Author & Date

Paul was released from prison in Rome around A.D. 63. He most likely went on his fourth missionary journey at that time. He was imprisoned again under Emperor Nero in A.D. 66 or 67. Paul wrote his second letter to Timothy during this time. Paul knew that his life was almost over. He was now in a cold and lonely dungeon awaiting death.

Purpose

Paul wrote II Timothy for a number of reasons. He was lonely and wanted to see Timothy again. Twice in this letter He asked Timothy to come soon (4:9,21). Timothy was facing many hardships, including Paul's imprisonment. Paul wanted to encourage Timothy in the Lord. Paul wanted Timothy to carry on the work he had begun. Paul had come to the end and could say that he had kept the faith and finished the course God had given him. He finished his life well and wanted Timothy to finish well also. He wanted Timothy to receive a crown of righteousness from the Lord on that Day.

Message and Main Points

Paul's message to Timothy is summarized below chapter by chapter.

Chapter 1. Timothy, use the gift God gave you with confidence. Do not be ashamed of our Lord or of me. I am a prisoner, but I am not ashamed.

Chapter 2. Stay focused on your task. Soldiers, athletes and farmers receive a reward if they stay focused and persevere. If we endure suffering we will reign with Christ. Be a man that God can use. Don't quarrel with people. Be kind and gentle to all.

Chapter 3. There will be terrible times in the last days. People will be totally evil and corrupt. You will be persecuted, but continue in what you have learned from me and from the Scriptures, which are God-breathed.

Chapter 4. Preach the word faithfully and fervently because the time will come when people will reject the truth. My departure is near. I will receive a crown of righteousness from the Lord. Then Paul gave Timothy final instructions and greetings.

Outline of II Timothy

Paul's Challenge to Timothy:
Commit Yourself to the Lord and to His Ministry

Hear the Word of the Lord Today!

16 All Scripture is God-breathed and is useful for teaching, rebuking, correcting and training in righteousness, 17 so that the man of God may be thoroughly equipped for every good work.

II Timothy 3:16-17 NIV

We believe that the Bible is the Word of God. It was written by men who were inspired by the Holy Spirit. The Word of God is powerful and practical. It is useful to teach people the right way, to rebuke them when they go the wrong way, to correct them when they need correction and to train them to live the righteous life God desires. Through this process we are **equipped** for every good work. May God give you a heart of wisdom and a deep hunger for His Word.

Week 13, Day 1

Read Philemon 1. Focus on Philemon 1:8-11.

Read Philemon 1. Then focus on verse 1:8-11. Read these verses two or three times. Ask God to help you understand and to speak to your heart.

⁸ Therefore, although in Christ I could be bold and order you to do what you ought to do, ⁹ yet I appeal to you on the basis of love. I then, as Paul—an old man and now also a prisoner of Christ Jesus— ¹⁰ I appeal to you for my son Onesimus, who became my son while I was in chains. ¹¹ Formerly he was useless to you, but now he has become useful both to you and to me.

Philemon 1:8-11 NIV

Write down your thoughts, insights and observations below.
Meditation Question: Who was Philemon and who was Onesimus? What did Paul mean when he said he was appealing on the basis of love?

What is God saying to you through these verses?

How will you trust and obey Jesus today?

Write a short prayer.

Key Verse
I appeal to you for my son Onesimus,
who became my son while I was in chains.
Philemon 1:10

Week 13, Day 2

Read II Timothy 1. Focus on II Timothy 1:6-7.

Read II Timothy chapter 1. Then focus on verse 1:6-7. Read these verses two or three times. Ask God to help you understand and to speak to your heart.

⁶ For this reason I remind you to fan into flame the gift of God, which is in you through the laying on of my hands. ⁷ For God did not give us a spirit of timidity, but a spirit of power, of love and of self-discipline.

II Timothy 1:6-7 NIV

Write down your thoughts, insights and observations below.
Meditation Question: Are you timid or fearful to use the gifts God has given you? How can you fan the flame so that you can step out in faith and love?

What is God saying to you through these verses?

How will you trust and obey Jesus today?

Write a short prayer.

Key Verse

For God did not give us a spirit of timidity, but a spirit of power,
of love and of self-discipline.
II Timothy 1:7

WEEK 13, DAY 3

Read II Timothy 2. Focus on II Timothy 2:1-2.

Read II Timothy chapter 2. Then focus on verse 2:1-2. Read these verses two or three times. Ask God to help you understand and to speak to your heart.

¹ You then, my son, be strong in the grace that is in Christ Jesus. ² And the things you have heard me say in the presence of many witnesses entrust to reliable men who will also be qualified to teach others.

II Timothy 2:1-2 NIV

Write down your thoughts, insights and observations below.
Meditation Question: Who can you teach the things that you are learning to? Will that person be able to teach someone else?

What is God saying to you through these verses?

How will you trust and obey Jesus today?

Write a short prayer.

Key Verse

And the things you have heard me say in the presence of many witnesses entrust to reliable men who will also be qualified to teach others.

II Timothy 2:2

WEEK 13, DAY 4

Read II Timothy 3. Focus on II Timothy 3:14-17.

Read II Timothy chapter 3. Then focus on verse 3:14-17. Read these verses two or three times. Ask God to help you understand and to speak to your heart.

14 But as for you, continue in what you have learned and have become convinced of, because you know those from whom you learned it, 15and how from infancy you have known the holy Scriptures, which are able to make you wise for salvation through faith in Christ Jesus. 16All Scripture is God-breathed and is useful for teaching, rebuking, correcting and training in righteousness, 17so that the man of God may be thoroughly equipped for every good work.

II Timothy 3:14-17 NIV

Write down your thoughts, insights and observations below.

Meditation Question: How does the Word of God impact our lives?

What is God saying to you through these verses?

How will you trust and obey Jesus today?

Write a short prayer.

Key Verse
16 Scripture is God-breathed and is useful for teaching, rebuking, correcting and training in righteousness, 17so that the man of God may be thoroughly equipped for every good work.
II Timothy 3:16-17

WEEK 13, DAY 5

Read II Timothy 4. Focus on II Timothy 4:6-8.

Read II Timothy chapter 4. Then focus on verse 4:6-8. Read these verses two or three times. Ask God to help you understand and to speak to your heart.

⁶For I am already being poured out like a drink offering, and the time has come for my

departure. ⁷I have fought the good fight, I have finished the course, I have kept the faith.

⁸Now there is in store for me the crown of righteousness, which the Lord,

the righteous Judge, will award to me on that day—and not only to me,

but also to all who have longed for his appearing.

II Timothy 4:6-8 NIV

Write down your thoughts, insights and observations below.

Meditation Question: Imagine that you die and are standing before the Lord. How will you feel when He gives you the crown of righteousness?

What is God saying to you through these verses?

How will you trust and obey Jesus today?

Write a short prayer.

Key Verse

I have fought the good fight, I have finished the race, I have kept the faith.

II Timothy 4:7

Frequently Asked Questions

QUESTION: What if I read the entire chapter for a day and I do not have enough time to complete the study? What should I do when I cannot spend more than 15 minutes doing the daily study?

ANSWER: If your time is very limited, instead of reading the entire chapter in the beginning, go directly to the verses selected from the chapter to focus on for that day. Complete the study for those verses first. Then read the chapter later if you have time (on the train, just before going to sleep, etc.).

(This may be especially important for <u>mothers with young children</u> who struggle to find time to read the Bible.)

QUESTION: What should I do if I fall behind in the weekly schedule?

ANSWER: If you fall behind during the week, try to complete the studies on the weekend. However, if you get behind and cannot catch up, discuss the matter with your reading partner. If you are reading in a group of two or three people, you can consult with your friends and agree to take a few days to catch up so that everyone is on the same page.

If you are doing the study with a larger group, it may be best to skip forward to join the rest of the group so that you will be studying the same chapters. The group may decide to provide some catch-up weeks to allow everyone to catch up with the group.

QUESTION: What if I do not have time to do every step (Read, Write, Listen, Trust & Obey, Pray) in the daily study?

ANSWER: In order to actually do the daily Bible studies each day, **it is very important to WRITE** your response to each question. You can write your answers either in the book, in a separate notebook, or on your computer or phone. However, if you are unable to answer every question in the study, then do your best and answer as many questions as possible.

The purpose is not to complete an assignment for someone else to look at or to fulfill an obligation. The purpose is to grow in your love relationship with God. Disciples of Jesus are full of life, joy and passion about following Him. Make this your focus and your time in the Word will be fruitful.

QUESTION: How do I find the right person(s) to do this study with?

ANSWER: You must do Knowing God Bible Study together for it to have its greatest impact and effectiveness in your life. The most important thing is to pray and ask God to give you the right partner for this study. You should be friends and have a good relationship. Both of you must be hungry for God's Word and desire to grow in Christ. You must be willing to make your daily time with God a priority and commit yourselves to sharing with one another each week.

QUESTION: What if I feel depressed or guilty if I do not complete all of the Bible studies during the week?

ANSWER: Reject guilt, condemnation, and legalism. We are not trying to become righteous by religious works. We are righteous before God because of what Jesus did for us on the cross. We are saved by grace, not by works (Ephesians 2:8-9). He does not condemn us! However, He wants us to love Him with all of our heart, soul and mind. He wants us to obey His commands because we love Him. Love requires commitment.

You make commitments to do many things for your wife or husband because you love him or her. Your commitment to spending time with God daily should come out of your love for Him. He does not condemn you when you miss a day of Bible reading, but he does miss your fellowship. He loves you and wants you to love Him. If we love God we will want to spend time with Him.

John 1:12
Yet to all who received him, to those who believed in his name, he gave the right to become children of God. NIV

John 2:5
"Whatever he says to you, do it."

John 3:3
"I tell you the truth, no one can see the kingdom of God unless he is born again." NIV

John 4:24
"God is spirit, and those who worship him must worship in spirit and truth."

John 5:39-40
"You search the Scriptures, because you think that in them you have eternal life; and these are they which testify about me. Yet you will not come to me, that you may have life."

John 6:29
"This is the work of God, that you believe in him whom he has sent."

John 7:37
"If anyone is thirsty, let him come to me and drink!"

John 8:12
"I am the light of the world. He who follows me will not walk in the darkness, but will have the light of life."

John 9:3
"This man didn't sin, nor did his parents; but, that the works of God might be revealed in him."

John 10:27
"My sheep hear my voice, and I know them, and they follow me."

John 11:25
"I am the resurrection and the life. He who believes in me will still live, even if he dies."

John 12:3
The house was filled with the fragrance of the ointment.

John 13:34-35
"A new commandment I give to you, that you love one another. Just as I have loved you, you also love one another. By this everyone will know that you are my disciples, if you have love for one another."

John 14:21
"Whoever has my commands and obeys them, he is the one who loves me. He who loves me will be loved by my Father, and I too will love him and show myself to him." NIV

John 15:5
"I am the vine. You are the branches. He who remains in me and I in him bears much fruit, for apart from me you can do nothing."

John 16:13
"However when he, the Spirit of truth, has come, he will guide you into all truth, for he will not speak from himself; but whatever he hears, he will speak. He will declare to you things that are coming."

John 17:20-21
"Not for these only do I pray, but for those also who will believe in me through their word, that they may all be one; even as you, Father, are in me, and I in you, that they also may be one in us; that the world may believe that you sent me."

John 18:11
Jesus therefore said to Peter, "Put the sword into its sheath." The cup which the Father has given me, shall I not surely drink it?"

John 19:30
"It is finished."

John 20:31
But these are written, that you may believe that Jesus is the Christ, the Son of God, and that believing you may have life in his name.

John 21:16
"Simon, son of Jonah, do you love me?"

Philippians 1:21
For to me, to live is Christ and to die is gain.

Philippians 2:5
Your attitude should be the same as that of Christ Jesus. NIV

Philippians 3:7
I consider those things that were gain to me as a loss for Christ.

Philippians 4:6-7
In nothing be anxious, but in everything, by prayer and petition with thanksgiving, let your requests be made known to God. And the peace of God, which surpasses all understanding, will guard your hearts and your thoughts in Christ Jesus.

I John 1:9
If we confess our sins, he is faithful and just and will forgive us our sins and purify us from all unrighteousness. NIV

I John 2:10
Whoever loves his brother lives in the light, and there is nothing in him to make him stumble. NIV

I John 3:18
Dear children, let us not love with words or tongue but with actions and in truth. NIV

I John 4:8
Whoever does not love does not know God, because God is love. NIV

I John 5:13
I write these things to you who believe in the name of the Son of God so that you may know that you have eternal life. NIV

Romans 1:17
"The righteous shall live by faith."

Romans 2:29
He is a Jew who is one inwardly, and circumcision is that of the heart, in the spirit not in the letter; whose praise is not from men, but from God.

Romans 3:10
"There is no one righteous; no, not one."

Romans 4:20-21
Yet, looking to the promise of God, he didn't waver through unbelief, but grew strong through faith, giving glory to God, and being fully assured that what he had promised, he was also able to perform.

Romans 5:8
But God commends his own love toward us, in that while we were yet sinners, Christ died for us.

Romans 6:23
The wages of sin is death, but the gift of God is eternal life in Christ Jesus our Lord. NIV

Romans 7:15
I do not understand what I do. For what I want to do I do not do, but what I hate I do. NIV

Romans 8:6
The mind of sinful man is death, but the mind controlled by the Spirit is life and peace. NIV

Romans 9:30-32
The Gentiles, who did not pursue righteousness, have obtained it, a righteousness that is by faith; but Israel, who pursued a law of righteousness, has not attained it. Why not? Because they pursued it not by faith but as if it were by works. NIV

Romans 10:9
If you confess with your mouth, "Jesus is Lord," and believe in your heart that God raised him from the dead, you will be saved. NIV

Romans 11:36
For of him, and through him, and to him are all things. To him be the glory for ever! Amen.

Romans 12:21
Do not be overcome by evil, but overcome evil with good.

Romans 13:8
Owe no one anything, except to love one another; for he who loves his neighbor has fulfilled the law.

Romans 14:1
Accept him whose faith is weak, without passing judgment on disputable matters. NIV

Romans 15:7
Accept one another, then, just as Christ accepted you, in order to bring praise to God. NIV

Romans 16:27
To the only wise God be glory forever through Jesus Christ! Amen. NIV

I Timothy 1:17
Now to the King eternal, immortal, invisible, the only God, be honor and glory for ever and ever. Amen. NIV

I Timothy 2:5
For there is one God and one mediator between God and men, the man Christ Jesus. NIV

I Timothy 3:13
Those who have served well gain an excellent standing and great assurance in their faith in Christ Jesus. NIV

I Timothy 4:8
For physical training is of some value, but godliness has value for all things, holding promise for both the present life and the life to come. NIV

I Timothy 5:1-2
Do not rebuke an older man harshly, but exhort him as if he were your father. Treat younger men as brothers, older women as mothers, and younger women as sisters, with absolute purity. NIV

I Timothy 6:10
For the love of money is a root of all kinds of evil. NIV

II John 1:6
And this is love: that we walk in obedience to his commands. As you have heard from the beginning, his command is that you walk in love. NIV

III John 1:4
I have no greater joy than to hear that my children are walking in the truth. NIV

Ephesians 1:3
Blessed be the God and Father of our Lord Jesus Christ, who has blessed us with every spiritual blessing in the heavenly places in Christ. NIV

Ephesians 2:8-9
For by grace you have been saved through faith, and that not of yourselves; it is the gift of God, not of works, that no one would boast.

Ephesians 3:17-19
That Christ may dwell in your hearts through faith, to the end that you, being rooted and grounded in love, may be strengthened to comprehend with all the saints what is the width and length and height and depth, and to know Christ's love which surpasses knowledge, that you may be filled with all the fullness of God. NIV

Ephesians 4:32
And be kind to one another, tender hearted, forgiving each other, just as God also in Christ forgave you. NIV

Ephesians 5:19-20

Speak to one another
with psalms, hymns and
spiritual songs. Sing and
make music in your heart
to the Lord, always
giving thanks to God the
Father for everything,
in the name of our Lord
Jesus Christ. NIV

Ephesians 6:10

Finally, be strong in the
Lord and in his mighty
power. NIV

Philemon 1:10

I appeal to you for my
son Onesimus, who
became my son while I
was in chains. NIV

II Timothy 1:7

For God did not give us
a spirit of timidity, but a
spirit of power, of love
and of self-discipline.
NIV

II Timothy 2:2

And the things you have
heard me say in the
presence of many
witnesses entrust
to reliable men who will
also be qualified to
teach others. NIV

II Timothy 3:16-17

All Scripture is God-
breathed and is useful
for teaching, rebuking,
correcting and training in
righteousness, so that the
man of God may be
thoroughly equipped for
every good work. NIV

II Timothy 4:7

I have fought the good
fight, I have finished the
race, I have kept the
faith. NIV

ABOUT THE AUTHOR

James Millard is the founder of Sunrise International Ministries. He and his wife Masako have been missionaries in Japan since 1978. They have been involved in training and equipping workers and leaders in many countries in Asia since 1995. They are now involved in discipleship equipping in several countries in Europe. They have four adult children, eight grandchildren and counting!

Made in the
USA
Columbia, SC